You Really Should Read the Bible
Seven Reasons Why

Gregory Bennett

© Gregory Bennett 2023

Faithbuilders Publishing
49 Kingmere, South Terrace, Littlehampton,
BN17 5LD, United Kingdom

ISBN: 978-1-908154-69-9

British Library Cataloguing in Publication Data. A catalogue record for this book is available from the British Library

Unless otherwise stated all scripture quotation are taken from The Holy Bible, English Standard Version (ESV) is adapted from the Revised Standard Version of the Bible, copyright Division of Christian Education of the National Council of the Churches of Christ in the U.S.A. All rights reserved.

NIV are taken from Holy Bible, New International Version® Anglicized, NIV® Copyright © 1979, 1984, 2011 by Biblica, Inc.® Used by permission. All rights reserved worldwide.

Printed in the United Kingdom

Contents

Acknowledgements

I cannot thank Yahweh—the God of the Bible—enough for everything he has done for me. I will be thanking him for all eternity. And I will thoroughly enjoy doing so.

I also thank my dear friend and brother in Christ, James Bejon, whose help has meant that I have been able to finish this book. He has devoted much time to this project. And his expertise in both the Bible and in editing has improved the book greatly.

My writing has also been heavily influenced by the teaching of many people, most notably Peter Williams (in the sections on New Testament names and the honesty of historical narratives), William Lane Craig (in the section on the proof of God's existence through objective morality), David Shaw (in the section about the Prodigal Son), Jacob Prasch (in the section on Joseph as a type of Christ), and Arnold Fruchtenbaum (in the section on Messiah Ben Joseph).

I thank my sisters in Christ, Chris Stevens, Anna Bennett and Jane Bejon for their eagle-eyed proofreading of my manuscript, their pertinent suggestions, and their words of encouragement.

I also thank Gareth Lucas for his excellent artwork and cover design. I do hope people will judge my book by its cover!

Finally, I thank wholeheartedly all the believers at my church, Collier Row Gospel Hall, for their many encouragements as I was writing this book.

Introduction

I spent many hard years as a young adult, making many bad choices along the way. I believed in God all that time. I just had no real sense of who he was, and what he expected from me. Had someone given me a book like this one at that time, it could have potentially saved me a lot of anguish and heartache.

My goal is not to make a robust defence of the Bible to sceptics. Rather, my goal is to show people who have a weak belief in God (like I had) that despite the unparalleled amount of criticism that the Bible receives, it is very much worth reading. It is a book like no other.

I hope, then, that my book will encourage people who already have some sympathy with the Christian faith to take a step towards the God of Christianity by reading his Bible for themselves.

I will provide seven reasons (chapters 2-8) why I believe the Bible is worth reading, and I hope that they will persuade readers of my book to become daily readers of the Bible. As I said, had I, in my young adulthood, been given a book that elevated the Bible, and encouraged me to read it, I would have saved myself a lot of pain. I want to save other people from much of that pain.

But my book is not just about pain-relief. I wholeheartedly believe that everyone would benefit from both reading and believing the Bible. That said, as I wrote, I had three particular groups of people in mind:

- seekers after God;
- Christians who want to confirm their faith in God and the Bible; and
- people who might historically have been against Christianity, but who now, having seen the way the West has drifted in this post-Christian era, wonder whether there might have been something in the Bible's message after all.

I think that all three groups would benefit from reading the Bible. And in this book I will provide seven good reasons for doing so.

ONE

The Effect of Believing the Bible

I became a Christian on Thursday 9th November 2000 at about 9:30pm. Before that day I would have called myself a Christian (I was a Catholic from birth). But I didn't genuinely believe the Bible. Yes, I believed in God's existence, and I even believed that Jesus walked the earth and was the Son of God. But if the Bible said something that didn't fit with the way I regarded the world—i.e. with my worldview—I was very happy to consider the Bible rather than my worldview to be wrong.

Truth be told, I didn't really have much of an idea what the Bible said about anything—Catholics don't tend to read the Bible—but occasionally in my pre-conversion days I encountered people who *genuinely* believed the Bible, and, even though I would have called myself a Christian, I quickly found myself in an opposing camp when they defended positions that went against my worldview.

I remember staying at the house of some friends of my then girlfriend. They were American evangelicals and they suggested to me that God had created the world in the six days described in Genesis Chapter 1. I thought they were crazy, and argued against everything they said. Believing the

Bible in its entirety wasn't very appealing to me if it lumped me together with those kind of nutcases.

I also had a very modern view of sex. I had the popular view that anyone was entitled to do whatever they wanted sexually with whomever they wanted, so long as they were both (or all!) consenting adults.

These are just a couple of areas in which, when push came to shove, I sided against the teachings of the Bible.

After my conversion I became convinced that the Bible was true, and, as a result, I now lead a very different life to the life I lived prior to November 2000.

For example, for most Saturdays in the last twenty years I have gone out to the local marketplace (initially in St Albans, but for the last 16 years, after moving there, in Romford, Essex) and I have preached a Christian message in the street. I have given out hundreds of portions of the Bible and many thousands of leaflets containing a Christian message. I have paid for the vast majority of these out of my own pocket. This is not normal behaviour. And to be honest, it is sometimes quite daunting to go out and preach. Very often I face some kind of opposition—mostly mockery, sometimes anger, and the odd threat of physical harm (although thankfully I never have been hit). So why do I do it?

Well, as I said, it is because I now believe the Bible. And that means I believe all of it. I can't pick and choose the bits I want to believe. Either it is the word of God, or it isn't. If it is, then I have to do whatever it tells me to do, even if I don't have a natural desire to do so. After all, it has been written by Almighty God, not by a mere man.

If you stick with me and read more of this book, you'll hopefully realise that the Christian message isn't one that comes naturally to any of us. It's something that goes against our natural understanding and desires. So, it's something that needs to be explained to people. As the Apostle Paul said in his letter to the Romans (10:14), 'How are they to believe in him of whom they have never heard? And how are they to hear without someone preaching?' God's message needs to be conveyed to people who would otherwise be unaware of it, and preaching is God's preferred means of doing so. It is this that motivates me to do something that I would never have considered before my conversion, i.e. to be a street preacher.

Not every Christian has the gift of preaching, of course, so not all Christians become street preachers. But I learned early on in my Christian walk that I did have that gift. So, street preaching on a Saturday is one way that believing the Bible has changed the way I live. (Before becoming a Bible believer, I used to spend most Saturdays nursing a hangover, until at some point in the day, my Saturday night drinking would start.) I don't want to go into all of the changes that have taken place in my life, but hopefully you will appreciate that genuinely believing the Bible will mean change for you.

You might not become a street preacher; you might not be a heavy drinker now. But if you end up believing the Bible, something would be quite wrong if it didn't result in a changed life.

I've already told you that I want to save you some pain, which I do, but I don't want to give the impression that life as a Christian is easy. The change in lifestyle can in fact be quite challenging. Lots of Christian books try and encourage conversion by speaking about the benefits of a changed life. And there is certainly a place for testimonies of drug addicts, gamblers and even murderers who have been miraculously born again and who now lead liberated and righteous lives. But I would also like to warn you to 'count the cost' (Luke 14:28) of ultimately becoming a Bible believer. The change to your life might well lead you to do things you wouldn't previously have dreamed of. And many of those things might be quite difficult for you.

So, I'm not promising you an easier life by becoming a Christian. After all, probably not many of you reading this are drug addicts, and so being liberated from an addiction isn't your main concern. But I am writing about a change of huge proportions.

If you become a genuine Bible believer, much of what you once valued will lose its lustre, and much of what you once ridiculed will become so precious to you that you would be willing to be killed for it. At the same time, everything in your life will have to be subordinated to Jesus' desires.

Subordinating your life to another person's plan for you isn't an easy thing to do. It is a sad indictment on mankind that the Frank Sinatra song, *I Did It My Way*, is played at many funerals. People want to celebrate the fact that they spent their life seeking to put themselves, rather than others, first. However, I believe that the greatest thing that could be said of me at my funeral was that I did things Jesus' way, not my own selfish way. And doing things Jesus' way, whilst being wonderfully rewarding and liberating, comes at a cost. You are likely to lose friends. You might lose your job. In many countries you might lose your life.

And it's this cost that Jesus speaks of when he warns us to 'count the cost' in Luke 14. Many people don't want to live in obedience to the teachings of the Bible. But I'm hoping you are still, at this stage, open to the possibility that an all-knowing God knows better than you what the best way to lead your life is.

Speaking personally, although there have been some great hardships in my Christian walk, I wouldn't trade it for anything. As the Apostle Peter said when Jesus asked him whether he wanted to leave him, 'Lord, to whom shall we go? You have the words of eternal life' (John 6:68). I agree. I can't find anything, anywhere in the world, that comes close to what I have with Christ. And I trust that God's plans for my life are much better than the plans I would make myself.

So, in my book, I'll take you through seven pieces of evidence for the truth of the Bible and I'll finish with a chapter on how to read the Bible effectively yourself. Perhaps none of the pieces of evidence is, on its own, enough to convince you of the truth of the Bible, but my hope is that you will give each chapter a fair hearing, and that together they will convince you to become a Bible believer too.

TWO

It is Supernaturally Put Together

At age 27 I started attending a church and reading the Bible every day. Before long I became amazed at how the Bible fitted together. I wasn't yet a Christian, but I could see that the Bible wasn't an ordinary book. It was written over many centuries, by many different writers, and yet there were themes that were intricately woven throughout the whole work.

I was no longer certain (after many years of leading a godless lifestyle) that there even was a god, and if there was one, whether he was the God of the Bible, but I quickly became convinced that whoever had written the Bible was worth following. What do I mean by that? Well, it became clear to me, due to the intricacy of themes running throughout the Bible, that there was an overarching author or editor (or editors) who had made the whole thing consistent, despite its many writers. I wondered at that time whether the editor/author could be an alien life form, or even a very inspired human or group of humans. But whoever had managed the compiling of the entire Bible was clearly an incredible intellect, and I had a strong desire to get to know them better.

I will endeavour in this chapter to give some sense of that intricacy of message. I won't be able to do it justice—I've been reading the Bible every day for more than 20 years by now, and I continue to learn more about its intricacy every day. I will only be able to concentrate on three areas: typology, the names of the people in the Bible, and prophecy. There are many other areas I *could* discuss, but hopefully these three will be sufficient to demonstrate the integrated and intricate nature of scripture as a whole.

Typology

The Bible is made up of two main sections: the Old Testament, which was written in Hebrew by Jews and primarily *for* Jews, and a New Testament, written again by Jewish authors, but this time in Greek because much of what was written was aimed at a Gentile audience.

It has been said that if you had to sum up the Old Testament in one word, 'Messiah' would be a good choice. The Old Testament promises a Messiah. The state of the world was such that a Messiah was needed, and only when he came would things get better.

But what even is a Messiah? And if we could sum up the Old Testament with the word, Messiah, why is that word not used in the Old Testament?

The Old Testament promises a wonderful future for God's people, and it says that this future will ultimately be brought in by an 'anointed' servant, which is what Messiah means— 'anointed'. Just as King Charles III was anointed with oil at his coronation, people who were singled out for a special purpose in the Bible were anointed.

But although the kings of Israel were anointed people, none of them was able to usher in this wonderful future—not even the greatest of them, such as David, who defeated all of Israel's enemies, or Solomon, who was considered the wisest of all the kings.

So, the Old Testament looks forward to a greater anointed one, who will bring in Israel's glorious future. By way of illustration consider one of the Old Testament passages that is read out at Christmas services:

> 'For to us a child is born,
> to us a son is given;
> and the government shall be upon his shoulder,
> and his name shall be called
> Wonderful Counsellor, Mighty God,
> Everlasting Father, Prince of Peace.
>
> Of the increase of his government and of peace
> there will be no end,
> on the throne of David and over his kingdom,
> to establish it and to uphold it
> with justice and with righteousness
> from this time forth and for evermore.
> The zeal of the Lord of hosts will do this.'
> (Isaiah 9:6-7)

So, this one who would come would sit on David's throne. And unlike the kings that went before him, he would succeed in setting up the predicted perfect kingdom. This figure is commonly called the Messiah.

If you could sum up the Old Testament with the word 'Messiah', what word might you choose to sum up the New Testament? Since the whole focus of the New Testament is on Jesus, the word 'Jesus' would be a natural choice. The Old Testament promises a Messiah, and the New Testament presents him to us. So, you can sum up the whole Bible in two words—Messiah and Jesus—or more commonly said, Jesus Christ (since Christ is the Greek word for Messiah).

However, while Jesus is *the* Messiah, there are many messianic figures who precede him. And typology is the study of the way they 'typify' him.

But God's plan of salvation is not a simple one, and so there are many facets to the life and mission of the Messiah. For example, for centuries, Jewish rabbis have wrestled with the idea that the Messiah of the Old Testament is portrayed in two quite contrasting ways. One way he is portrayed is as a reigning king, and the other way he is portrayed is as a suffering servant. The Christian's solution to the riddle is a Messiah who comes twice. The first time that he came, Jesus suffered greatly. When he comes again, he will reign as a king.

The greatest example of a king in the Old Testament is David (who defeated Israel's enemies, wrote many of the Psalms, and was described by God as 'a man after his own heart': 1 Samuel 13:14). And so the rabbis call the kingly Messiah *Ha Mashiach Ben David*—Messiah the son of David. They then call the Messiah who suffers *Ha Mashiach Ben Yoseph*—Messiah the son of Joseph.[1] The rabbis

---

[1] These suffering-related prophecies were probably associated with a descendant of Joseph due to the text of Genesis 49.

themselves did not expect there to be direct correlations between Joseph's life and the Messiah's, and so, perhaps they didn't fully appreciate the significance of the name they chose for the suffering Messiah, but as we will see now, Joseph's life had many similarities to Christ's.

Joseph as a type of Christ

Joseph's story is recounted in the latter chapters of the first book of the Bible, Genesis. It was also made into an Andrew Lloyd-Webber musical called *Joseph and the Amazing Technicolour Dreamcoat*, so Joseph is one of the better-known characters from the Bible.

Let's consider how similar Joseph's experiences were to those of Jesus, the later literal son of Joseph (the carpenter).

Joseph was initially betrayed by his brothers into the hands of Gentiles. He was sold into slavery for 20 pieces of silver. Sometime later the price of a slave was set at 30 pieces of silver (see Exodus 21:32), which is the price at which Jesus was sold.

The key instigator of Joseph's betrayal was his brother Judah. The New Testament equivalent of that name is Judas, and it was Judas who infamously betrayed Jesus. God took that betrayal and turned it into an opportunity for all Israel and the world to be saved. So Joseph saved Israel from famine (discussed below), and Christ saves Israel (and the world) from sin.

Like Christ, Joseph was falsely accused of a crime, and was thrown in prison. He was imprisoned with two other people—a baker and a cupbearer. And just like the two criminals crucified at the same time as Jesus, where one put his faith in Christ and was saved while the other didn't, one of Joseph's fellow prisoners was set free while the other wasn't.

But, just like Christ on the day of his resurrection, Joseph was raised up from his place of condemnation (prison) to a place of authority in a single day. He was given all authority in the land of Egypt, second only to Pharaoh.

As Prime Minister, Joseph organised a plan to save the world from upcoming famine. His own brothers then came to him when the famine struck, seeking food. When they met him the first time, they didn't recognise him. They weren't expecting to see their brother, surrounded by Gentiles (i.e. non-Jews). They assumed him to be a foreigner. But the second time they met him, they did recognise him, and wept. Similarly, Jesus' Jewish brethren did not recognise him for who he was the first time he came. But the prophet Zechariah tells us that the Jewish people will 'weep bitterly over him, as one weeps over a firstborn' (Zechariah 12:10) when he comes the second time. Because Jesus' Jewish brethren largely rejected him, he wedded himself to a mostly Gentile bride (the Church is called the bride of Christ). Similarly, Joseph married a Gentile.

There are plenty of other parallels between Joseph's life and Christ's (see *Gleanings in Genesis* by Arthur W. Pink), but hopefully these examples show that there was more than a passing resemblance between the original Joseph and the later son of Joseph.

Moses as a type of Christ

But Joseph was not the only Old Testament person to 'typify' Christ. The very next deliverer to arise after Joseph was Moses. And Moses, like Joseph, also lived a life that prefigured Christ's life.

Moses was born about four hundred years after Joseph. By that time, there was a new Pharaoh ruling in Egypt, and, unlike his predecessor, he was not well-disposed towards the Jews who lived there. This new Pharaoh was involved in many events which are fulfilled in Christ. One of them is the slaying of innocent infant boys.

Many people are familiar with Herod's attempt to kill the infant Christ after his birth. A similar thing happened at the time Moses was born—Pharaoh had ordered the killing of all male new-born Jews. But Moses was saved from this fate when his mother left him in a 'Moses basket' in the reeds of the Nile. He was then found, picked up, and raised by Pharaoh's own daughter.

As Moses's life continues, so do the parallels between his life and Christ's. Moses, like both Joseph and Jesus, was initially rejected as leader of the Jewish people. He then spent forty years in the wilderness, and at that time he too took a Gentile bride. Only on his return to Egypt was he received by the Jewish people as their leader. In the same way, the Jews will one day receive Christ as their leader and Messiah, which they will do when he returns, i.e. at his second coming (see Romans 11).

Another event that is fulfilled in Christ is the Passover. Moses called down ten plagues on the people of Egypt, and it was only after the tenth plague that Pharaoh was finally willing to let Moses's people leave Egypt where they had been slaves. That tenth plague involved the Angel of Death's slaughter of all the firstborn sons in the land. But God told the Jews that they could protect themselves by painting the blood of a sacrificed lamb on their doorposts. This was the first Jewish Passover, which acquired its name because the Angel of Death 'passed over' all the Jewish homes that were protected by the blood of the lambs.

Many centuries later, John the Baptist described Jesus as the 'Lamb of God who takes away the sin of the world' (John 1:29). I, and all other born-again believers, are protected from God's wrath against sin. We are protected not by a lamb's blood as in that first Passover, but by the blood of Jesus which was shed at the cross, exactly on the day of the Jewish festival of Passover.

Just as it took the death of the firstborn sons of Egypt to set the Israelites free from Egypt, so it took the death of God's son (sometimes called the firstborn, by virtue of his position of prominence; see Colossians 1) to set the world free from sin.

Moses also prefigured Christ in that in Exodus 32 he was willing to be killed in place of his people who had sinned so grievously against God that he wanted to destroy them. God declined Moses's offer, but he accepted Christ's. Christ himself is the ultimate substitute—in his death he was punished for our sin so that we don't have to be.

Isaac as a type of Christ

Joseph and Moses were two major deliverers who point towards the ultimate deliverer, Christ. Other characters from the Old Testament typify him in other ways. Many people have heard of Abraham. He was the father of the Jewish people (and the great grandfather of Joseph). It was with him, for example, that God made a covenant symbolised by circumcision.

Abraham's son was Isaac. And since Abraham is portrayed as a prototypical father in the Bible, Isaac is portrayed as a prototypical son. It is in this aspect of his sonship that Isaac prefigures Jesus.

In a striking story in Genesis 22, Abraham is instructed to sacrifice Isaac, his 'only son' (verse 2), as a burnt offering. Isaac is then laid upon wood (as Christ was put on a wooden cross), and Abraham, in an incredible demonstration of his faith, is about to sacrifice his son when God tells him to stop, and gives him a ram to sacrifice instead.

God hates pagan human sacrifice. He strongly criticised the Canaanites for this very practice (e.g. Deuteronomy 12:31), so he had never intended Abraham to actually sacrifice Isaac. But the incident showed Abraham's incredible faith. More importantly for our current study, it prefigured God the Father's ultimate sacrifice of God the Son, and importantly, their combined willingness to go through with it.

There are many more characters in the Old Testament who foreshadow Christ in some way, and much has been written on the topic (see for example *The Study of the Types* by Ada Habershon). These three examples, however, should be sufficient to demonstrate the intricacy and cohesion of the text of scripture, not to mention God's control over history. The people I have told you about actually lived, and their lives, written about centuries before Christ, bear remarkable similarities to Christ's own life. We are not, therefore, dealing with random Nostradamus-esque phrases, some of which might have a little bit of significance in some situation many years later. We are dealing with real events—the lives of real people—written about many years before Christ walked on the earth, and they wonderfully speak of the very life that Jesus would live.

The names of people in the Bible

Imagine you were set the task of writing a story set in 19th century England, i.e. between 100 and 200 years ago. How would you know what names to give your characters? I am English, and I have some reasonably elderly friends with names like Ivy, Iris and Gladys. I could guess that those three names were also popular a hundred years before my friends were born, but perhaps they weren't. I also have the internet at my disposal, so I could carry out some research that would uncover quite a few more names.

Imagine, however, that you were trying to write the Bible centuries after its events happened (as many people claim— we'll see why they do so in the next section on prophecy), with no internet, and perhaps in a completely different country. How on earth would you come up with all the names in the Bible?

Over 2000 individuals' names occur in the Bible, and when you look into them, they turn out to be appropriate to their dates and locations. That would be quite a feat to achieve if the stories were made up at quite a distance in time and location from the time and location in which they are set.

Let me give you some examples to show you what I mean. At the time of the Gospels and the book of Acts, i.e. in about the middle third of the first century AD, the most popular two names for Jewish men in Israel were Joseph and Simon. These two names account for 16% of recorded male names, while in the Gospels and Acts they account for 18%. The bigger picture reveals similar findings—the top nine most popular names in Israel at that time make up 42% of recorded male names, compared to 40% in the Gospels and Acts.[2]

These are rather striking correlations, especially when you consider that in Jewish communities outside Israel, male names were quite different.[3] Recording the truth is clearly a lot easier to get right than making up stories! Remember— some would like to argue for a large gap in distance and time between what the Bible describes and when it was written.

The Bible's accuracy in name usage is also reflected in its use of disambiguation. What do I mean by that? If a headline in a UK newspaper were to read tomorrow, 'Boris found guilty of cheating,' there would be no doubting who was being written about. There aren't terribly many people called Boris in UK public life, so there is no need to provide

---

[2] Richard Bauckham, *Jesus and the Eyewitnesses: The Gospels as Eyewitness Testimony* (Wm B Eerdmans Publishing Co 2008) as cited in Peter J Williams, *Can We Trust the Gospels?* (Crossway Books 2018).

[3] Peter J Williams, *Can We Trust the Gospels?* (Crossway Books 2018) 66.

a surname. We would all know it was referring to the former Prime Minister, Boris Johnson. However, if the headline read, 'David found guilty of cheating,' the headline writer might end up getting the sack for failing to get his message across clearly! There are many Davids in UK public life, and without some sort of disambiguation, we can't guess who is being referred to.

Similarly, in Jesus' day, some names were so common that they needed some form of disambiguation so that people would know who was being talked about. The name 'Jesus' was just such a name, being the sixth or seventh most popular name in Israel when Jesus walked the earth. That fact is borne out in the New Testament. Every single time direct speech is recorded as mentioning Jesus, some form of disambiguation is included, e.g. 'The crowds answered, "This is Jesus, the prophet from Nazareth in Galilee"' (Matthew 21:11), or 'Now Peter was sitting out in the courtyard, and a servant girl came to him. "You also were with Jesus of Galilee," she said' (Matthew 26:69). (NB surnames as we know them now didn't exist in 1st century Israel, so the means of disambiguation varies.)

So when the exact words that people said are recorded by the Gospel writers, they always include disambiguation. And yet, whenever Jesus is written *about* in the Gospels or anywhere else in the New Testament there is no need for any disambiguation, because everyone knows exactly which Jesus is being referred to, and so no disambiguation is necessary.

The same principle is neatly borne out in the list of the twelve disciples. In this list below from Matthew's Gospel, the popularity rank of each name in first century Israel has been added inside square brackets. As you can see, the most popular names were disambiguated, but there was no need to do so with the less popular names:

> 'The names of the twelve apostles are these: first, Simon [1], *who is called Peter*, and Andrew [outside the top 100] his brother; James [11] *the son of Zebedee*, and John [5] his brother; Philip [61] and Bartholomew [50]; Thomas [outside the top 100] and Matthew [9] *the tax collector*; James [11] *the son of Alphaeus*, and Thaddaeus [39]; Simon [1] *the Zealot*, and Judas [4] *Iscariot*, who betrayed him.' (Matthew 10:2-4)

When I became a Christian, I realised that I had to stop lying. Lying, and in particular embellishing stories to make me look better, had been such a large part of my existence that this was quite a drastic change. The wonderful thing about always telling the truth is that it is very uncomplicated. There's nothing that you need to remember to say to one person that fits in with other things you've told him; you just tell the truth. I no longer, therefore, need to remember what I've told to whom. There's no pressure on me to make sure my stories all match. My housemate would say that the downside to this is that I now quickly forget what stories I've told him in the past, and so I have become rather repetitive!

This principle that recording the truth is simple to do is worth remembering when thinking of the appropriateness of the disambiguation in the Gospels. It would have been very hard to achieve an accurate portrayal of the names of the characters in the Gospels if they were made up after the events. It is relatively easy, however, to accurately record the names of people you have met.

So far we have only considered New Testament names. But plenty of research has been carried out on Old Testament names as well, and it too attests to the reliability of scripture.

One rather attractive testimony to the accuracy of the Old Testament's names concerns the way that names were chosen for new-borns. The Old Testament is made up of 39 individual books, written by a variety of different authors over a long span of time, and most of these books contain names of specific individuals. Some books contain only a handful of names, others contain many long lists. And yet all of them reflect an unusual naming custom—that children weren't named after characters from Israel's history. There is, for example, only one Abraham, only one Moses, only one Isaac, and so on.

Things are very different today. My brothers and I were all named after popes. And today, it is common to name a new-born after someone else, be it a parent, other relative, or famous person (hence there was an increase in babies being named Winston after the Second World War). At the time of the New Testament, the situation in Israel was much the same. John the Baptist was expected to be named after his father, and many people bore the names of Israel's past heroes, e.g. Simon, Judas (which were both names of sons of Jacob), etc. Even the name Jesus is just an anglicisation of the name, Joshua (and Joshua was the man who led the Israelites into the Promised Land).

This naming custom is only reflected in the Biblical text after the Jews have been conquered and led away to

Babylon. Perhaps it was motivated by a desire to give children very Jewish names given that they were in a foreign land, surrounded by foreign people. By giving themselves very Jewish names, they might have felt that they could maintain their Jewish identity better.

Either way, according to the Biblical text, a change in naming customs occurred around the 5th century BC. And the archaeological record reflects exactly the same state of affairs. More than 3000 artefacts with names on them from the time and place of the Old Testament have been found. And, while pre 5th century artefacts don't bear the names of famous individuals, post 5th century names do, especially as we approach the time of the New Testament.

As I have already said, it is worth stressing that producing an accurate record of historical names is no easy task. Unless I got lucky, I wouldn't be able to choose five appropriate names from my own country 100-200 years ago. And yet the Bible's names, of which there are thousands, covering different millenniums and locations, follow a consistent and independently verifiable pattern. Either they are the actual names of the people who lived, recorded in the Biblical text by authors who were contemporaries of the relevant individuals, or later authors were somehow able to reconstruct a vast and historically plausible record of names many years after the relevant events. As we will see in the next section on prophecy, there are reasons why people want to believe the latter scenario (that the Bible was written many years after the events portrayed in the text). But it is far easier to believe in authors who simply recorded the names of their contemporaries in an accurate fashion.

Prophecy

The Bible is the only religious book that dares to authenticate itself through prophecy. Close to one third of the Bible's text is prophetic in nature. God says through Isaiah the prophet, 'I am God, and there is no other; I am God, and there is none like me, declaring the end from the beginning and from ancient times things not yet done' (Isaiah 46:9-10).

Prophecy has two main focal-points. Both of them describe the coming of the Lord into the world. As we noted earlier, Jews today tend to view these two comings as one event, while Christians have a first coming around two thousand years ago and look forward to a second coming sometime in the future.

In what follows, I will look at some prophecies relating to both Jesus' first coming and his second coming. I will also look at some prophecies that don't relate to either coming of Christ, but that have nevertheless been fulfilled in history. These are important because they validate the Bible as a book that can predict the future.

Prophecies of Christ's first coming

Many facts about Jesus' first coming were predicted in the Old Testament. For example, Micah 5:2 says, 'But you, O Bethlehem Ephrathah, who are too little to be among the clans of Judah, from you shall come forth for me one who is to be ruler in Israel, whose coming forth is from of old, from ancient days.' Just as there is more than one place called Stratford in England (hence Stratford-upon-Avon), there was more than one place in Israel called Bethlehem. This verse predicted that a 'ruler in Israel' would come specifically from the Bethlehem that was in Ephrathah (i.e. within the territory of the tribe of Judah). It also suggests that that ruler would have existed before he came forth from Bethlehem in that he was 'from of old, from ancient days.' And it's worth pointing out that it's not only Christians who understand Micah 5:2 this way; Jewish rabbis, who had no desire to authenticate Jesus' Messianic claims, also did so.

So, Jesus fulfilled Micah's prophecy. He was born in Bethlehem. But as is often the case with Jesus, things are more complicated than they first seem—that is, there was more to Jesus' origin than being born in Bethlehem.

Bethlehem wasn't Jesus' home. He only happened to have been born there after his parents had to return to Bethlehem because of a census that took place at the time of his birth. Jesus actually grew up in Nazareth, which is why he was often referred to as the Nazarene. And, remarkably, this confusion concerning the Messiah's origins was prophesied.

In Isaiah 11:1, it was predicted that a 'shoot' would 'come forth' from the royal line of King David. And yet later, in Isaiah 53:2, it was predicted that a 'shoot' (many translations have the word 'root' instead of 'shoot', but the Hebrew is the same in Isaiah 11 and 53) would come 'out of dry ground' and would have 'no form or majesty'.

So, on the one hand, the Messiah would be of a royal line, born in a royal city, and yet, on the other, he would have no form of majesty—in other words, he would not look much like a king. Jewish rabbis, including notably Maimonides, have picked up on this confusion and have said, like the people in John 7:27, 'When the Christ appears, no one will know where he comes from.' So, Jews (who, by the way, have no reason to want to affirm Jesus' Messianic claims) have a view that the Messiah's origins will be a bit confused. He will not be obviously majestic, but will come from a kingly line. All this is explained by Jesus' birth in Bethlehem, coupled with his being raised by a lowly carpenter in the backwater of Nazareth.

It is very important to stress at this point that we have copies of the Old Testament that are older than Joseph and Mary. I have enjoyed visiting the Shrine of the Book in the Israel Museum in Jerusalem, where, for example, a scroll of the whole book of Isaiah is on display. Jewish scholars, who have no theological reason to want to date it before Christ was born in Bethlehem, date the scroll to around 100 BC.

I have spoken to many people who want to reject the Christian message, and as a result they often object to prophecies about Christ's first coming. They casually toss them away with comments like, 'Well, the Bible was written after Jesus' birth.' But we have Old Testament manuscripts today (e.g. the Dead Sea Scrolls) which predate Christ's first coming. In which case, the many prophecies about Christ in the Old Testament need to be taken seriously.

Many things were prophesied about the Messiah in addition to the nature of his coming, but I don't want to get bogged down in them in this short book. (If you want to consider Old Testament prophecies of Christ further, Michael Brown's *Answering Jewish Objections to Jesus: Volume 3: Messianic Prophecy* would be a great book to read.) For now, all I would like to make you consider is Isaiah 53, in which Christ's purpose and mission is predicted. Have a read of it and see whether you can see Christ and his suffering for the sin of mankind predicted there.

Before you read it, it is worth noting that Biblical prophetic writing is often written as if a particular person or group of people is speaking. These people are often engaged in an imaginary conversation in a future setting. With that in mind, try and think about who is speaking, who they are speaking to, and who they are speaking about. The clearest way to read the passage, to my mind, is to take the people speaking (i.e. the 'us', and the 'we') to be Jews who have finally come to realise that the person they are speaking about is Jesus (i.e. most of the references to 'he'/'him'), who is in fact the Messiah (something they didn't previously think). There is also another 'he' that appears in places, and I would suggest that that 'he' is God the Father.

> 'Who has believed what he has heard from us? And to whom has the arm of the Lord been revealed?
>
> For he grew up before him like a young plant, and like a root out of dry ground; he had no form or majesty that we should look at him, and no beauty that we should desire him.
>
> He was despised and rejected by men; a man of sorrows, and acquainted with grief; and as one from whom men hide their faces he was despised, and we esteemed him not.
>
> Surely he has borne our griefs and carried our sorrows; yet we esteemed him stricken, smitten by God, and afflicted.
>
> But he was wounded for our transgressions; he was crushed for our iniquities; upon him was the

chastisement that brought us peace, and with his stripes we are healed.

All we like sheep have gone astray; we have turned—every one—to his own way; and the Lord has laid on him the iniquity of us all.

He was oppressed, and he was afflicted, yet he opened not his mouth; like a lamb that is led to the slaughter, and like a sheep that before its shearers is silent, so he opened not his mouth.

By oppression and judgement he was taken away; and as for his generation, who considered that he was cut off out of the land of the living, stricken for the transgression of my people?

And they made his grave with the wicked and with a rich man in his death, although he had done no violence, and there was no deceit in his mouth.

Yet it was the will of the Lord to crush him; he has put him to grief; when his soul makes an offering for guilt, he shall see his offspring; he shall prolong his days; the will of the Lord shall prosper in his hand.

Out of the anguish of his soul he shall see and be satisfied; by his knowledge shall the righteous one, my servant, make many to be accounted righteous, and he shall bear their iniquities.

Therefore I will divide him a portion with the many, and he shall divide the spoil with the strong, because he poured out his soul to death and was numbered with the transgressors; yet he bore the sin of many, and makes intercession for the transgressors.' (Isaiah 53:1-12)

I personally see Jesus all over these verses, especially since I know about the very purpose of Christ's death, as explained in the New Testament. In chapter 4 of this book, I will discuss the central message of Christianity, which is often called 'the Gospel'. Perhaps, once you've read that chapter, you could re-read Isaiah 53. I'm hoping that you too will see Christ's sacrifice for sin clearly predicted in it.

Prophecies of Christ's second coming

Although there are many prophecies *about* Christ, there are also many prophecies that Christ himself made. Many of the things he said refer to the state of the world when he will return, e.g. Matthew 24, Luke 21, Mark 13. Much of what Christ prophesied in those passages concerns things that have always taken place—e.g. natural disasters, pestilences, wars—so they aren't so remarkable. However, there is a suggestion in scripture that these things will increase in intensity and frequency like labour pains (see Matthew 24:8 and 1 Thessalonians 5:3). And it could be argued that natural disasters, wars and pestilences have indeed increased in both intensity and frequency. Of course, I can understand that some people will not be persuaded by this, yet the New Testament predicts even that reaction, since the Apostle Peter refers to people who will view the tumultuous events leading up to Jesus' return as business as usual. 'Scoffers will come in the last days with scoffing', Peter says, 'following their own sinful desires. They will say, "Where is the promise of his coming? For ever since the fathers fell asleep, all things are continuing as they were from the beginning of creation"' (2 Peter 3:3-4).

Given, then, that many people are likely to view prophecies of wars and the like as nothing out of the ordinary, I would like to talk about a couple of prophecies that concern things which clearly *are* out of the ordinary, and which would have seemed quite strange to be predicting in the 1st century.

Firstly, John wrote in Revelation that there would be one 'beast' (sometimes called the False Prophet) who would 'cause all, both small and great, both rich and poor, both free and slave, to be marked on the right hand or the forehead, so that no one can buy or sell unless he has the mark, that is, the name of the beast or the number of its name' (Revelation 13:16-17). This prophecy is clearly speaking of all people needing a mark of some sort on their hand or forehead in order to be able to buy or sell.

For most of history, such a state of affairs would have seemed impossible to bring about, but we can now, for the first time, see how it could be done. Jews and escaped prisoners, evading the Nazis in the Second World War, could be given fake papers and cash so that they could survive. Yet our society is moving ever closer to a world in which governments can prevent people from buying and selling altogether—the kind of control Hitler could only have dreamed of. Digital currency is very easy to turn on and off. And we saw during the Coronavirus pandemic that some people (specifically non-vaccinated people) could be and were prevented from entering certain venues (including in some instances grocery stores). Whatever your personal take is on vaccine passports, the fact is that we now have the technology, and the political will—in an emergency—to prevent a subsection of society from engaging in activities as basic as shopping.

Today, then, we can easily imagine the kind of society that is predicted by John, and yet, 2000 years ago, John could hardly have done so. How did he know to write such things? Was it a very good guess? Or could he have been informed by someone who 'knows the end from the beginning' (Isaiah 46:10)?

Another significant prophecy is that at the time of the end, i.e. the coming of Christ, Jerusalem would be at the very centre of the world's concerns. Zechariah wrote, speaking on behalf of God:

> 'Behold, I am about to make Jerusalem a cup of staggering to all the surrounding peoples. The siege of Jerusalem will also be against Judah. On that day I will make Jerusalem a heavy stone for all the peoples. All who lift it will surely hurt themselves. And all the nations of the earth will gather against it.' (Zechariah 12:2-3)

So, Jerusalem would be a 'cup of staggering' and 'a heavy stone for all the peoples.' And, as prophesied, Jerusalem and Israel are now on the receiving end of almost more scrutiny by the United Nations than the rest of the world put together. Yet when Zechariah penned his prophecy, how influential a city was Jerusalem? True, some Jews had returned from their captivity in Babylon by the time of Zechariah's writing, but it was really anything but an impressive city. After all, Nehemiah had to plead with his fellow Jews to return to it. It was a minnow of a city.

Yet, today, the whole world seems to be concerned with Jerusalem. It is not inconceivable to imagine a time when 'all the nations of the earth will gather against it.' Israel becomes more isolated and more criticised on the world stage with every year that passes.

Again, then, unlike wars and the like, Jerusalem being a 'heavy stone for all the peoples' is not something that has always been the case. Only since its rebirth in 1948 has Israel become a problem for all the nations. And, interestingly, that very rebirth was foretold in scripture. For example, Ezekiel said, speaking for God, 'I will bring you out from the peoples and gather you out of the countries where you are scattered, with a mighty hand and an outstretched arm, and with wrath poured out' (Ezekiel 20:34). It is not hard to see the holocaust as a part of this very regathering, i.e. 'with wrath poured out.'

But are Christians just reading Israel's rebirth back into scripture? Not necessarily. Many Christians, notably the Puritans of the 17th century and well-known later Christians such as Charles Spurgeon and Robert Murray M'Cheyne, predicted Israel's rebirth long before it happened because they understood the Bible to predict it. Similarly, many Christians have been expecting there to be a cashless society for many years because it seems to be what the Bible predicts. And now that too seems to be coming true.

Are these prophecies merely coincidence, or could the Bible truly be written by God through the penmanship of men?

Prophecies of other historical events

Some people object to prophecies about Christ's first coming on the basis that we only have scripture (the New Testament) to know that these prophecies did in fact come true. The same people also object to prophecies of his second coming because they have not yet fully come to pass.

But the Bible contains some prophecies that *have* fully come to pass and that we *do* have an independent historical record of.

For example, the prophet Daniel wrote a lot about the time between the two testaments. It was a very important time in world history, with the rise of Alexander the Great and his Greek empire, followed ultimately by the Roman empire, which was in full swing by the time Jesus was born.

Daniel did much of his writing during the Babylonian empire and during the beginnings of the Persian empire in the 6th century BC. Towards the end of his time of writing he wrote the following words:

> 'Behold, three more kings shall arise in Persia, and a fourth shall be far richer than all of them. And when he has become strong through his riches, he shall stir up all against the kingdom of Greece. Then a mighty king shall arise, who shall rule with great dominion and do as he wills. And as soon as he has arisen, his kingdom shall be broken and divided towards the four winds of heaven, but not to his posterity, nor according to the authority with which he ruled, for his kingdom shall be plucked up and go to others besides these.' (Daniel 11:2-4)

The three kings that were to arise after Cyrus (the king in Daniel's day) were Cambyses, who reigned between 530-522 BC, Smerdis (522 BC), and Darius I (522-486 BC). That makes the fourth king Xerxes, who invaded Greece in 480 BC with an army of over one million men. (His invasion included the famous battle with the 300 Spartans.)

The 'mighty king' who arises in the third sentence then naturally fits the career of Alexander the Great, who rapidly conquered a vast domain and died at a young age, leaving his empire to be divvied up between four of his generals rather than his descendants, as Daniel prophesied.

The chapter goes on to describe these four parts of his empire with such accuracy that many people claim it was written after the event. The logic goes like this: Daniel predicts the future; no-one can predict the future; so Daniel must have been written after its 'predictions' came true.

Armed with this logic, critical scholars have come up with a scheme where the bulk of Daniel's prophecies were written in 164 BC, but were presented to the Jewish people as if they'd been written centuries earlier in order to encourage them in their time of trial. (The Jews were being persecuted by a Greek king named Antiochus.) The encouragement would stem from the fact that the writings demonstrated that they served a living God who was able to predict the future.

This, however, is to take a rather low view of the Jewish people. How could someone convince the Jews of 164 BC that a book written in the 6th century BC had predicted the last few centuries' events with unerring accuracy but they'd somehow not heard about it or read it before? And, if the Jews couldn't be convinced of such a thing, but knew that Daniel was written after the event, then why would they be encouraged by it? The Jews went to great lengths to preserve scripture, even though that very scripture was often, as we will see in chapter 6, scathingly critical of them as a people. They treasured the word of God. Why, then, would those same Jews happily include something in their canon that they knew was made up after it claimed to have been written?

It seems to me that critical scholars simply cannot allow for the possibility that God exists, and that he does indeed know the end from the beginning. With that as a starting point, there is little hope of convincing them that the Bible contains genuine prophecy. Everything will be explained away somehow. It is also worth remembering the intricacy and accuracy of the names in the Bible. The names contained in the book of Daniel fit the 6th century BC. That would have been easy for Daniel to get right had he been alive at the time. It would have been much harder for a 2nd century author to get right.

My hope is that you will be more open-minded than these critical scholars, and will allow for the possibility that God could know the future. I also hope that these few prophecies that I've written about might make you open to the possibility that the Bible is no ordinary book.

As I said at the start of the chapter, when I started reading the Bible, I was blown away by the cleverness and intricacy of its message. Hopefully, thinking about typology, the names within the Bible, and the prophecies within the Bible might start to convince you too that the Bible is worthy of being read. And maybe, this intricacy combined with other reasons I give later on for why you should read the Bible will encourage you to read it too.

THREE

Its Moral Quality is Unparalleled

One of the first books I read in the Bible was the Gospel of Matthew, which is the first book in the New Testament. I felt that I already had a reasonable knowledge of the first couple of chapters because they contain many passages that are read at Christmas services. Chapter 3 then introduces John the Baptist. I had heard of him, so, again, this seemed familiar to me. And chapter 4 has the temptation of Jesus, which was something that I was already aware of.

What followed next were three chapters taken up with one of Jesus' sermons, called the Sermon on the Mount. I had heard small parts of it before, but had never read the whole thing in one go. When I did, I was simply amazed by the moral quality of the teaching. I am keen for you to have a similar experience, so I have included the full text of those three chapters below.

Many people will not agree with all of Jesus' teaching in this sermon (we'll see why in the next chapter), but I think most people would have to admit that a society run exclusively on the principles taught in it would be morally superior to most, if not all, societies in history. A society with no hypocrisy, anger or adulterous desires, but instead, love for others, humility and the desire to sort oneself out before criticising others, would be a truly fine society.

I thought about trying to give some commentary alongside Jesus' words, but I think the sermon has greater impact if you just read it as it is. I have, however, included the headings that the English Standard Version (which is the version I have quoted throughout this book) of the Bible includes. Bibles often have headings in them to aid readers. Those headings aren't a part of the original text of scripture, so they are different in different translations of the Bible.

If you feel happy to, I would encourage you to ask God to speak to you through the words you read. Prayers need not be complicated, and truthfulness is always more important than grand-sounding words. Something as simple as 'Dear God, if you are there at all, please do show me something in these words,' would be a very nice request to make. Often prayers end with an 'Amen', but they don't need to if you think it sounds a bit too religious. God knows what you mean, and whether you are sincere, irrespective of the actual words you use.

* * * * *

The Sermon on the Mount

Seeing the crowds, he went up on the mountain, and when he sat down, his disciples came to him.

The Beatitudes

And he opened his mouth and taught them, saying:

"Blessed are the poor in spirit, for theirs is the kingdom of heaven.

"Blessed are those who mourn, for they shall be comforted.

"Blessed are the meek, for they shall inherit the earth.

"Blessed are those who hunger and thirst for righteousness, for they shall be satisfied.

"Blessed are the merciful, for they shall receive mercy.

"Blessed are the pure in heart, for they shall see God.

"Blessed are the peacemakers, for they shall be called sons of God.

"Blessed are those who are persecuted for righteousness' sake, for theirs is the kingdom of heaven.

"Blessed are you when others revile you and persecute you and utter all kinds of evil against you falsely on my account. Rejoice and be glad, for your reward is great in heaven, for so they persecuted the prophets who were before you.

Salt and Light

"You are the salt of the earth, but if salt has lost its taste, how shall its saltiness be restored? It is no longer good for anything except to be thrown out and trampled under people's feet.

"You are the light of the world. A city set on a hill cannot be hidden. Nor do people light a lamp and put it under a basket, but on a stand, and it gives light to all in the house. In the same way, let your light shine before others, so that they may see your good works and give glory to your Father who is in heaven.

Christ Came to Fulfil the Law

"Do not think that I have come to abolish the Law or the Prophets; I have not come to abolish them but to fulfil them. For truly, I say to you, until heaven and earth pass away, not an iota, not a dot, will pass from the Law until all is accomplished. Therefore whoever relaxes one of the least of these commandments and teaches others to do the same will be called least in the kingdom of heaven, but whoever does them and teaches them will be called great in the kingdom of heaven. For I tell you, unless your righteousness exceeds that of the scribes and Pharisees, you will never enter the kingdom of heaven.

Anger

"You have heard that it was said to those of old, 'You shall not murder; and whoever murders will be liable to judgement.' But I say to you that everyone who is angry with his brother will be liable to judgement; whoever insults his brother will be liable to the council; and whoever says, 'You fool!' will be liable to the hell of fire. So if you are offering your gift at the altar and there remember that your brother has something against you, leave your gift there before the altar and go. First be reconciled to your brother, and then come and offer your gift. Come to terms quickly with your accuser while you are going with him to court, lest your accuser hand you over to the judge, and the judge to the guard, and you be put in prison. Truly, I say to you, you will never get out until you have paid the last penny.

Lust

"You have heard that it was said, 'You shall not commit adultery.' But I say to you that everyone who looks at a woman with lustful intent has already committed adultery with her in his heart. If your right eye causes you to sin, tear it out and throw it away. For it is better that you lose one of your members than that your whole body be thrown into hell. And if your right hand causes you to sin, cut it off and throw it away. For it is better that you lose one of your members than that your whole body go into hell.

Divorce

"It was also said, 'Whoever divorces his wife, let him give her a certificate of divorce.' But I say to you that everyone who divorces his wife, except on the ground of sexual immorality, makes her commit adultery, and whoever marries a divorced woman commits adultery.

Oaths

"Again you have heard that it was said to those of old, 'You shall not swear falsely, but shall perform to the Lord what you have sworn.' But I say to you, Do not take an oath at all, either by heaven, for it is the throne of God, or by the earth, for it is his footstool, or by Jerusalem, for it is the city of the great King. And do not take an oath by your head, for you cannot make one hair white or black. Let what you say be simply 'Yes' or 'No'; anything more than this comes from evil.

Retaliation

"You have heard that it was said, 'An eye for an eye and a tooth for a tooth.' But I say to you, Do not resist the one who is evil. But if anyone slaps you on the right cheek, turn to him the other also. And if anyone would sue you and take your tunic, let him have your cloak as well. And if anyone forces you to go one mile, go with him two miles. Give to the one who begs from you, and do not refuse the one who would borrow from you.

Love Your Enemies

"You have heard that it was said, 'You shall love your neighbour and hate your enemy.' But I say to you, Love your enemies and pray for those who persecute you, so that you may be sons of your Father who is in heaven. For he makes his sun rise on the evil and on the good, and sends rain on the just and on the unjust. For if you love those who love you, what reward do you have? Do not even the tax collectors do the same? And if you greet only your brothers, what more are you doing than others? Do not even the Gentiles do the same? You therefore must be perfect, as your heavenly Father is perfect.

Giving to the Needy

"Beware of practising your righteousness before other people in order to be seen by them, for then you will have no reward from your Father who is in heaven.

"Thus, when you give to the needy, sound no trumpet before you, as the hypocrites do in the synagogues and in the streets, that they may be praised by others. Truly, I say to you, they have received their reward. But when you give to the needy, do not let your left hand know what your right hand is doing, so that your giving may be in secret. And your Father who sees in secret will reward you.

The Lord's Prayer

"And when you pray, you must not be like the hypocrites. For they love to stand and pray in the synagogues and at the street corners, that they may be seen by others. Truly, I say to you, they have received their reward. But when you pray, go into your room and shut the door and pray to your Father who is in secret. And your Father who sees in secret will reward you.

"And when you pray, do not heap up empty phrases as the Gentiles do, for they think that they will be heard for their many words. Do not be like them, for your Father knows what you need before you ask him. Pray then like this:

"Our Father in heaven, hallowed be your name. Your kingdom come, your will be done, on earth as it is in heaven. Give us this day our daily bread, and forgive us our debts, as we also have forgiven our debtors. And lead us not into temptation, but deliver us from evil.

For if you forgive others their trespasses, your heavenly Father will also forgive you, but if you do not forgive others their trespasses, neither will your Father forgive your trespasses.

Fasting

"And when you fast, do not look gloomy like the hypocrites, for they disfigure their faces that their fasting may be seen by others. Truly, I say to you, they have received their reward. But when you fast, anoint your head and wash your face, that your fasting may not be seen by others but by your Father who is in secret. And your Father who sees in secret will reward you.

Lay Up Treasures in Heaven

"Do not lay up for yourselves treasures on earth, where moth and rust destroy and where thieves break in and steal, but lay up for yourselves treasures in heaven, where neither moth nor rust destroys and where thieves do not break in and steal. For where your treasure is, there your heart will be also.

"The eye is the lamp of the body. So, if your eye is healthy, your whole body will be full of light, but if your eye is bad, your whole body will be full of darkness. If then the light in you is darkness, how great is the darkness!

"No one can serve two masters, for either he will hate the one and love the other, or he will be devoted to the one and despise the other. You cannot serve God and money.

Do Not Be Anxious

"Therefore I tell you, do not be anxious about your life, what you will eat or what you will drink, nor about your body, what you will put on. Is not life more than food, and the body more than clothing? Look at the birds of the air: they neither sow nor reap nor gather into barns, and yet your heavenly Father feeds them. Are you not of more value than they? And which of you by being anxious can add a single hour to his span of life? And why are you anxious about clothing? Consider the lilies of the field, how they grow: they neither toil nor spin, yet I tell you, even Solomon in all his glory was not arrayed like one of these. But if God so clothes the grass of the field, which today is alive and tomorrow is thrown into the oven, will he not much more clothe you, O you of little faith? Therefore do not be anxious, saying, 'What shall we eat?' or 'What shall we drink?' or 'What shall we wear?' For the Gentiles seek after all these things, and your heavenly Father knows that you need them all. But seek first the kingdom of God and his righteousness, and all these things will be added to you.

"Therefore do not be anxious about tomorrow, for tomorrow will be anxious for itself. Sufficient for the day is its own trouble.

Judging Others

"Judge not, that you be not judged. For with the judgement you pronounce you will be judged, and with the measure you use it will be measured to you. Why do you see the speck that is in your brother's eye, but do not notice the log that is in your own eye? Or how can you say to your brother, 'Let me take the speck out of your eye', when there is the log in your own eye? You hypocrite, first take the log out of your own eye, and then you will see clearly to take the speck out of your brother's eye.

"Do not give dogs what is holy, and do not throw your pearls before pigs, lest they trample them underfoot and turn to attack you.

Ask, and It Will Be Given

"Ask, and it will be given to you; seek, and you will find; knock, and it will be opened to you. For everyone who asks receives, and the one who seeks finds, and to the one who knocks it will be opened. Or which one of you, if his son asks him for bread, will give him a stone? Or if he asks for a fish, will give him a serpent? If you then, who are evil, know how to give good gifts to your children, how much more will your Father who is in heaven give good things to those who ask him!

The Golden Rule

"So whatever you wish that others would do to you, do also to them, for this is the Law and the Prophets.

"Enter by the narrow gate. For the gate is wide and the way is easy that leads to destruction, and those who enter by it are many. For the gate is narrow and the way is hard that leads to life, and those who find it are few.

A Tree and Its Fruit

"Beware of false prophets, who come to you in sheep's clothing but inwardly are ravenous wolves. You will recognize them by their fruits. Are grapes gathered from thorn bushes, or figs from thorn bushes? So, every healthy tree bears good fruit, but the diseased tree bears bad fruit. A healthy tree cannot bear bad fruit, nor can a diseased tree bear good fruit. Every tree that does not bear good fruit is cut down and thrown into the fire. Thus you will recognize them by their fruits.

I Never Knew You

"Not everyone who says to me, 'Lord, Lord', will enter the kingdom of heaven, but the one who does the will of my Father who is in heaven. On that day many will say to me, 'Lord, Lord, did we not prophesy in your name, and cast out demons in your name, and do many mighty works in your name?' And then will I declare to them, 'I never knew you; depart from me, you workers of lawlessness.'

Build Your House on the Rock

"Everyone then who hears these words of mine and does them will be like a wise man who built his house on the rock. And the rain fell, and the floods came, and the winds blew and beat on that house, but it did not fall, because it had been founded on the rock. And everyone who hears these words of mine and does not do them will be like a foolish man who built his house on the sand. And the rain fell, and the floods came, and the winds blew and beat against that house, and it fell, and great was the fall of it."

The Authority of Jesus

And when Jesus finished these sayings, the crowds were astonished at his teaching, for he was teaching them as one who had authority, and not as their scribes.
(Matthew 5-7)

* * * * *

Reading the Bible is different from reading other books. There are many levels at which the text can be understood. In the final chapter I will give some basic teaching on how to read the Bible effectively, but the main thing to do if you want to know what the Bible says is simply to read it. That seems obvious, but it is worth emphasising. You can't learn what the Bible says without reading it. I am no longer surprised at the lack of knowledge of the Bible that people in England have. Amazingly, though, I often speak to people who *think* they know the Bible well, and yet really don't.

I would suggest, as a simple rule for Bible reading, that if you want to understand a text better, you should read it multiple times. So, you might like to read this sermon again at some point. In the meantime, I hope you were able to see some of the beauty of Jesus' words. They blew me away the first time I read them, and they seemed to affect his listeners similarly (as the last sentence says). I don't think that Jesus' teaching will ever be surpassed for its moral quality. Of course, not everyone *agrees* with Jesus' teaching. As we'll discuss in the next chapter, it's often preferable to come up with our own standard of morality—one that's more convenient than Jesus'. But this isn't a good thing.

FOUR

Its Explanation of Morality, Sin and Justice is Unrivalled

Why are we so concerned with how people behave? Pick up a newspaper and you will find numerous articles about the poor behaviour of some sportsman or politician, or someone who regularly calls for action on climate change but flies around in a private jet.

Discussing morality sells newspapers. We make a big deal about immoral behaviour. If someone has behaved badly, we want it publicly known, and we want some kind of retribution to take place. The Bible gives a good explanation for why this is so.

Mankind is different from animal kind. In the Bible's account of creation, after God has made the animals, we read that:

> 'God said, "Let us make man in our image, after our likeness. And let them have dominion over the fish of the sea and over the birds of the heavens and over the livestock and over all the earth and over every creeping thing that creeps on the earth."

So God created man in his own image, in the image of God he created him; male and female he created them.

And God blessed them. And God said to them, "Be fruitful and multiply and fill the earth and subdue it and have dominion over the fish of the sea and over the birds of the heavens and over every living thing that moves on the earth.'" (Genesis 1:26-28)

So, man was special. Unlike the animals that he was to have dominion over, he was made in the image of God. This is a radically different view of man to the common Darwinian view, which holds that man is just an advanced animal.

But what does it mean to be made in God's image? It means many things. God is a creator, and so mankind likewise has creative abilities, which animals do not. More relevantly to the issue at hand, God is a moral judge, and so man likewise is moral. We are concerned with right and wrong in a way that animals simply aren't.

The Bible also teaches us about our role as decision-makers. Our original parents, Adam and Eve, were able to choose to behave well or badly, and unfortunately, they chose to do the one thing that God had told them not to—they ate the fruit of the 'tree of the knowledge of good and evil' (Genesis 2-3). With that act came grave consequences. Death was introduced into the world, and through eating the fruit, man was able to discern good from evil. Ever since, as a species, we have been extremely concerned with the rightness or wrongness of moral actions. But, rather than accepting God's standard of good and evil, we have all too often come up with our own. To come up with our own standard of morality isn't a straightforward thing to do. Because we have been made in God's image, and because he has given each of us a conscience, we often know deep down that something is wrong, even when many people tell us it is fine. That said, we are able to sear our consciences (1 Timothy 4:2) and, worse still, we are able to defile our consciences (Titus 1:15). We can convince ourselves that something that an unseared conscience would deem morally bad is not actually morally bad, and sometimes we can even convince ourselves that it is morally good.

I can't help but think that this is sadly exemplified in the way that many people champion killing unborn babies in the womb. I was recently listening to the radio presenter Andrew Castle reporting on the statistic that, nowadays, over a quarter of pregnancies in the UK end in abortion. He said that he didn't want to make any particular judgment about the matter, but that he found the statistic incredibly sad. As far as I am aware he is not a Christian, but his reaction was a Christian one. The person whom he was interviewing, however, immediately replied, 'Not as sad as becoming pregnant and then being forced to go through with the pregnancy.' Apparently, nothing about the statistic struck her as sad. I find that hard to explain in any way other than that she has a seared conscience.

Sometimes someone starts telling me something that I don't want to know—e.g. information about the end of a film that I haven't yet seen, or the score of a rugby match before I've seen the highlights—and when I hear them start to give the game away, I start to make a lot of noise to drown out whatever they're saying. I can't help but view the very loud support for abortion in some quarters to be doing a similar thing—it is deadening consciences.

Maybe you are personally supportive of abortion. I don't want to dwell on that particular issue in this chapter—I just want to point out that, at various points in history, societies have convinced themselves that something is good, when in actual fact it is immoral. Cannibalistic societies are a good example of this. They convinced themselves that killing and eating humans was good. Nazi Germany was a similar society, with its 'Final Solution' to eradicate the Jews in the Second World War promoted as a great good. People in these societies had seared their consciences to such an extent that they 'call[ed] evil good and good evil' (Isaiah 5:20).

A brief aside to discuss an argument for God's existence—the Moral Argument

The fact that we are moral agents is a remarkable aspect of our existence, and, as we'll see in this section, it points to the existence of an ultimate Moral Agent.

Most people would agree that the Final Solution was objectively morally wrong. What I mean by that is that the Final Solution would have been wrong even if Hitler had won the war and convinced the rest of the world to go along with him. Whether or not people *thought* it was good, it was still morally wrong.

Some people, however, claim that moral choices are purely subjective. What that means is that the morality of actions are purely a matter of opinion. On such a view, determining whether something is wrong is akin to deciding whether you prefer apple crumble or cheesecake. Hitler wouldn't, therefore, be an objectively evil man; he would simply be a man with an unusual or unfashionable taste in morality.

Yet deep down, we all know that Hitler's Final Solution was objectively morally wrong. And other things fall into the same category. For example, raping and murdering defenceless infants is objectively wrong. It's not a matter of personal taste as to whether it is wrong. It just is.

As I mentioned earlier, the existence of an objective standard of morality is a good argument for the existence of God. The argument can be formulated as follows:

1. If God does not exist, objective moral values and duties do not exist.
2. Objective moral values and duties do exist.
3. Therefore, God exists

If we unpack each of these statements a bit, it will hopefully become clear that this is a good argument for God's existence. The first thing to note is that point 1 is often misunderstood. People think it says that *belief* in God is necessary for objective moral values to exist. But point 1 does not say, 'If *I believe* God does not exist, then objective moral values and duties do not exist'. Point 1 has nothing to do with whether or not someone believes in God's existence; rather, it states that without God as the objective source for moral values and duties, there aren't any. That is, if we are all made up simply of chemicals and time and random processes, then without God, we are without an objective standard of morality.

We would still probably want to define a standard of morality for the sake of convenience. For example, in order to protect the clan (and then later the society and country) we would want to define murder as wrong. But this kind of morality would be purely subjective, and would be motivated by convenience rather than truth. It would be similar to the UK's societal decision to drive on the left rather than the right—convenient but ultimately arbitrary.

Remarkably, however, many Atheists affirm the view I have just described—that the morality that we as a society have developed is ultimately arbitrary. As Charles Darwin wrote in *The Descent of Man*, 'If ... men were reared under precisely the same conditions as hive-bees, there can hardly be a doubt that our unmarried females would, like the worker-bees, think it a sacred duty to kill their brothers, and mothers would strive to kill their fertile daughters; and no one would think of interfering.'[4]

Again, point 1 isn't stating that only people who believe in God can be moral people. Belief has nothing to do with it. What point 1 is stating is that, without God as a source of moral values, man can only come up with morals himself—subjectively.

And yet, as point 2 states, some things are just wrong. Even if the whole world were to tell you that raping defenceless infants was not morally wrong, you would still know full well that it was. So objective moral values and duties do exist. In which case the conclusion of the argument follows (point 3): God exists.

---

[4] Charles Darwin, *The Descent of Man and Selection in Relation to Sex* (2nd edn, D Appleton & Company 1909) 100, as quoted in William Lane Craig, *On Guard: Defending Your Faith with Reason and Precision* (David C Cook 2010) 132.

Some people will no doubt still bite the bullet and say that there are no objective moral truths, but they do so, I believe, solely in order to reject God's existence. They are not sincere seekers after truth. A man who can convince himself that rape is not morally wrong can convince himself of anything.

This book, however, is not intended to provide proof of God's existence, so we will not discuss the moral argument any further here. To learn more about it, and other arguments for the existence of God, please take a look at the work of William Lane Craig, especially the books *On Guard* and *Philosophical Foundations For a Christian Worldview*.

Returning to the Bible's dealing with man's morality

So what, according to the Bible, is the upshot of us having a moral nature? Like many other religions, the Bible speaks of a day of judgment where every man and woman will be judged according to how they have lived their lives:

> 'Then I saw a great white throne and him who was seated on it. From his presence earth and sky fled away, and no place was found for them. And I saw the dead, great and small, standing before the throne, and books were opened. Then another book was opened, which is the book of life. And the dead were judged by what was written in the books, according to what they had done.' (Revelation 20:11-12)

Some people recoil from the idea of a judgment. I recently attended a funeral in which the Vicar told everyone present that the deceased was definitely in heaven, and that we would all see him again when we died, since all of us were guaranteed to go to heaven. This kind of message appeals to some people. If heaven exists, we all want to end up there, so the temptation is to tell ourselves we all will, and be done with it. Easy.

Unfortunately, many people who call themselves Christians are proponents of precisely such a message. This type of preaching leads Atheists to think that Christianity is simply wishful thinking. And I agree with them—*that* kind of message is indeed wishful thinking. More importantly, it is completely unbiblical. The Vicar I mentioned did a real disservice to his audience. He failed to warn them that, according to the Bible, many people will be judged unfavourably in the final judgment. Heaven is not a guarantee. In fact, the Bible teaches us that the majority of people will be judged unfavourably. For example, Jesus said:

> 'Enter by the narrow gate. For the gate is wide and the way is easy that leads to destruction, and those who enter by it are many. For the gate is narrow and the way is hard that leads to life, and those who find it are few.' (Matthew 7:13-14)

According to the Bible, then, a judgment awaits us all. And when we stop to think about it, the Bible's teaching is far more appealing to us as moral creatures than the idea that there is no judgment at all. Insofar as we are made in the image of God, we have a sense of justice. If Hitler, after everything he did, is now enjoying the same blissful existence as the millions he killed, then something very unjust will have happened.

When the paedophile atrocities that Jimmy Saville had carried out during his life came to light after his death, people were horrified. It seemed as if he had got away with what he had done. But not according to the Bible. We are promised a 'day when God judges people's secrets through Jesus Christ' (Romans 2:16, NIV). 'Nothing is covered up that will not be revealed, or hidden that will not be known' (Luke 12:2).

God has seen everything we have ever done, or even wanted to do. All of it—all of those daily moral decisions we make—will be judged. And the clear teaching of the Bible is that, in fact, the majority of us are on the wide road 'that leads to destruction'. So, what do we need to do to avoid destruction? No question is more important for us to be able to answer than this.

Well, as I said above, Christianity is very much like other religions insofar as it says that we will be judged on the basis of how well we have behaved. However, the pass mark for heaven, according to the Bible, is very different from what is prescribed by all other religions. Jesus told us to 'be perfect, as your heavenly Father is perfect' (Matthew 5:48). And this was just after saying, 'Love your enemies and pray for those who persecute you...For if you love those who love you, what reward do you have? Do not even the tax collectors do the same? And if you greet only your brothers, what more are you doing than others? Do not even the Gentiles do the same?' (Matthew 5:44; 46-47).

The pass mark for heaven, then, is perfection, and Jesus gives us an example of what that looks like—loving our enemies and those who persecute us. It's easy to love those who love you. But Jesus expects something much better than that from us—quite literally, moral perfection. Elsewhere, he puts it in a comparative way, saying, 'I tell you that unless your righteousness surpasses that of the Pharisees and the teachers of the law, you will certainly not enter the kingdom of heaven.' (Matthew 5:20). These Pharisees and teachers of the law were considered the most righteous people of all. Today, we might say that unless someone's righteousness surpasses that of Mother Teresa, he will not enter the kingdom of heaven.

Of course, Jesus' 'pass mark' is impossible to attain, but at least it is clear and non-arbitrary. By contrast, most other religions hold to a vague notion that our good deeds and bad deeds will somehow be weighed up and assessed, but nobody knows what the pass mark is. Could it be 60%? Or 70%? Who knows?

Nevertheless, lots of people think this way. They hope that on the day of judgment they will have done enough to withstand God's scrutiny, but they have no idea of exactly how much good they need to have done. This is a desperate situation. How unreasonable of the gods of these non-Biblical religions not to stipulate what the pass mark for heaven is. In each of my degrees I knew exactly what the pass mark was for every exam and every piece of coursework I wrote. If men can provide such information, why can't gods?

Catholicism offers a bit of extra help at this point. If you haven't quite been good enough, you can pay the shortfall in Purgatory. The problem is, no-one knows how long you will have to spend there. It is all desperately vague. With something so important as our eternal destiny, couldn't we expect a bit more certainty of the rules from God?

In contrast, the Biblical pass mark is clearly stated— perfection. No sin at all. And this pass mark is not arbitrarily chosen by God. It is the pass mark required by God's very character.

As human beings, we live in a world where sin is commonplace. We are so used to it that it doesn't offend us terribly much—we have all had our consciences seared and defiled to some extent. Granted, some sins are still rare enough and heinous enough that they offend us, but most of them just get shrugged off as part of life (after all, we commit those same sins ourselves). Yet God is so pure that any sin at all—no matter how insignificant it might seem given our sin-infused perception of the world—is an offence to him.

To get a sense of how seriously God views sin we can read these words of Jesus:

> 'And if your hand causes you to sin, cut it off. It is better for you to enter life crippled than with two hands to go to hell, to the unquenchable fire. And if your foot causes you to sin, cut it off. It is better for you to enter life lame than with two feet to be thrown into hell. And if your eye causes you to sin, tear it out. It is better for you to enter the kingdom of God with one eye than with two eyes to be thrown into hell.' (Mark 9:43-47)

As it happens, we would never be able to cut off enough body parts to become sinless. (The Bible teaches that our own heart is full of sinful desires—try cutting that off!) Jesus is not, therefore, teaching self-harm. He wants to show us just how serious sin is to God. That is why his pass mark for heaven is so high. Any sin at all is an offence to a perfectly good God. And, deep down, most of us recognise that there's something right and good about that.

Just as strict judgment is better than no judgment at all, as we saw above, so a perfect pass mark for heaven is better than a lower pass mark. If you or I could qualify for heaven having attained a score of 60% (whatever that would actually entail), what kind of a heaven would it be? It certainly wouldn't be a very special place, since it would be letting in rather mediocre people, i.e. people who are really quite sinful. The heaven that the Bible speaks about, by contrast, is unimaginably good. The Apostle Paul refers to heaven as

> '…what no eye has seen, nor ear heard, nor the heart of man imagined, what God has prepared for those who love him.' (1 Corinthians 2:9)

Paul's description of heaven recognises that we are not able to even guess what it will be like. Some people mock heaven by saying things like, 'Well, I wouldn't want to be stuck on a cloud playing a harp forever anyway.' But we have such limited imaginations. God has unimaginable wonders awaiting those who enter heaven.[5] Compared to the mediocre afterlifes of other religions, the Biblical heaven is wonderful. However, there is a big problem. Since 'all have sinned and fall short of the glory of God' (Romans 3:23),

---

[5] As a point of clarification, the Bible teaches that ultimately his people will dwell, not in heaven, but on a renewed earth, with resurrected, perfected bodies. However, at the moment, when Christians die, they go to heaven. In this context I am using the word heaven, but ultimately, I long for an unimaginably good eternity, dwelling bodily on a perfect earth.

how can sinners enter into a glorious heaven? God, who is perfect, can't lower his standards. If he did, he would no longer be perfect. So, what can be done? How on earth can sinners like us get into heaven?

God's perfect solution was to send his son into the world in order to pay the price of our entrance into heaven. Around thirty years after his birth in Bethlehem, Jesus Christ was crucified on a cross in Jerusalem. The whipping and the nails involved in his crucifixion would undoubtedly have been painful, and the fact that these cruelties were inflicted on him by the hands of his very own creation would certainly also have hurt. But something greater was happening. Jesus was being punished by God for *our* sins—for all the sins his creation had carried out in rebellion against him and the conscience he gave to us. John the Baptist described Jesus as 'the Lamb of God, who takes away the sin of the world' (John 1:29). And the Apostle John describes him as 'the propitiation for our sins' (1 John 2:2).

Jesus paid the price for the sins of the whole world on the cross. He was able to pay that price in full because he is God himself, i.e. because he is pure enough not to require punishment himself, and strong enough to bear the sins of the whole world. Nobody else would have been able to do this. No man; no angel; only God himself.

This means that the debt we owe God for our sins has already been paid, and so God can graciously offer us complete forgiveness. However, we don't automatically come into the good of this. God asks us to believe in Jesus, and to repent of our sin. But what exactly does belief and repentance entail?

Believing in Jesus is much more than just believing in his existence, or even that he is God (which is something that 'Even the demons believe': James 2:19). We need to believe that Jesus' work on the cross was necessary (because we are full of sin), and that his work on the cross is complete. If we truly believe this, then we will understand quite how serious sin is. It required the Son of God to be crucified, and that should make us repent of sin, i.e. try to avoid sin at all costs.[6]

We will see in the next chapter that while, in one sense, belief is easy, in another sense it is incredibly difficult because to believe the Gospel involves humility— something a lot of us find very hard to muster up. But, at the moment, all I want to focus on is the perfect way God has dealt with our sin. The Bible speaks of a perfect heaven, a perfect judgment, a world guilty before God, and a perfect saviour who paid the price. Through the cross, God can be both just (since all sin is punished) and merciful (since he forgives the sins of all who believe in his work).

If we could get into heaven with a 60% pass mark, then God would not be just. Even a 99% pass mark[7] would still leave sins outstanding which would need to be punished if God was to remain just. Yet, the God of the Bible has paid in full the price for all sin. And so, through the cross, God can be

---

[6] NB, people who carry on leading an unchanged, sinful life after 'believing', clearly haven't truly believed the full message. They haven't developed a God-inspired hatred of sin. A genuine conversion will lead to more holy living. If there are no obvious changes in a convert's life, the conversion itself ought to be questioned.

[7] And tempting as it might be for people to view their own 'mark' as closer to 99% than to an outright fail, the Bible's clear teaching is that we all fall well short of God's high standards. See Romans 3:10-18 for a damning verdict on all mankind.

both 'just and the justifier of the one who has faith in Jesus' (Romans 3:26).

Before we move on to the next chapter, it is worth considering one final aspect of the Gospel, namely what makes Jesus an appropriate person to judge us. Jesus not only knows all things, being God, but has experienced what it is like to live as a man, and so can make a perfect judgment: he is not someone 'who is unable to sympathize with our weaknesses, but one who in every respect has been tempted as we are, yet without sin' (Hebrews 4:15). He knows fully what life on earth is like. So, while human judges have to make do with incomplete knowledge, Jesus' judgment comes from a place of complete knowledge.

One of the reasons I believe the Bible, then, is that its message makes sense of our moral experiences, and offers the forgiveness we need without any compromise of justice. It gives reasons why morality matters so much to us. It proclaims a completely holy God with perfect standards, who will judge perfectly, and be fully just in so doing. It proclaims a totally merciful God who 'desires all people to be saved and to come to the knowledge of the truth' (1 Timothy 2:4), and who is also perfectly loving—'God shows his love for us in that while we were still sinners, Christ died for us' (Romans 5:8). God came and met us in our time of need. We were totally unpresentable to him—in fact, as sinners, we were his enemies—and yet it was precisely when we were in that state that he died for us (he truly showed us how to love our enemies). He just leaves us to, in humility, accept his message.

FIVE

It Appeals to the Humble

King Solomon wrote these words—'When pride comes, then comes disgrace, but with the humble is wisdom' (Proverbs 11:2). Jesus said a similar thing—'Blessed are the meek, for they shall inherit the earth' (Matthew 5:5). James, Jesus' brother, followed suit—'Humble yourselves before the Lord, and he will exalt you' (James 4:10). And the Apostle Paul wrote these words—'Do nothing from rivalry or conceit, but in humility count others more significant than yourselves' (Philippians 2:3).

Over recent decades, Western society has become less and less Christian. As a result, pride has come to be considered a virtue in some quarters. Not so to God, who 'opposes the proud but gives grace to the humble' (1 Peter 5:6). And well he might. Genuine humility is a beautiful thing, whereas pride and arrogance are often very unpleasant to witness. Moreover, humility is an appropriate state for us all to adopt. Even the greatest human minds know only a tiny fraction of the knowledge in the universe. As Aristotle famously said, 'The more you know, the more you realise you don't know.'

Furthermore, none of us really get what we deserve. Even self-made businessmen (so-called) have often had many 'lucky breaks' along the way. All of us have made terrible decisions at times, but have often got away with them (when other people seem not to have). And if we have had success in our lives, then although we may well have worked hard (which is, of course, a good thing), we will also have had many things beyond our control go just right. As a result, the Apostle Paul's words are very important to remember—'I say to every one among you not to think of himself more highly than he ought to think, but to think with sober judgement' (Romans 12:3).

One of the things that convinces me of the truth of the Bible is the way its message is most well-received by the humble, and not by the proud. When he was on earth Jesus had most success with the outcasts of society—prostitutes, tax collectors and the like. The big shots, on the other hand, e.g. the religious leaders and the political leaders, weren't interested in following his teachings. And this principle has held true throughout the centuries.

When I'm out street-preaching, I offer Christian leaflets to people to read. Sometimes this can be fairly disheartening to say the least, since most people in England don't want to hear about the Christian message. When I feel particularly disheartened, I look for encouragement by making a beeline with my leaflets for older black women.

There is a lot of discussion about privilege in society these days—some groups of people tend to get a better start in life than others. One group that has had more obstacles to face than most others is that of older black women. In Biblical terms this demographic might be referred to as being more 'lowly'. And interestingly, it tends to be more Christian than most. Often when I give a leaflet to an older black woman,

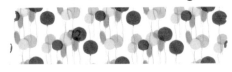

she says encouraging things to me in a way that is less common amongst, say, wealthy white men.

God has a particular love for the humble and the lowly. And the humble and the lowly are far more likely than the proud and self-important to choose to believe the Christian message. The Apostle Paul said in his first letter to the church at Corinth:

> 'For consider your calling, brothers: not many of you were wise according to worldly standards, not many were powerful, not many were of noble birth. But God chose what is foolish in the world to shame the wise; God chose what is weak in the world to shame the strong; God chose what is low and despised in the world, even things that are not, to bring to nothing things that are, so that no human being might boast in the presence of God.'
> (1 Corinthians 1:26-29)

Down the years, the Church has been full of the lowly of society. For example, in the Indian subcontinent, converts to Christianity very often come from the lowliest caste, the Untouchables, and far less commonly from the higher strata of Indian society. This principle can be observed in society after society, wherever the Bible and its message has gone.

Yet how do you write a book so that it appeals to the humble, but doesn't appeal to the proud? It is not an easy thing to do.

I don't claim to understand the incredible mind of God and how he has achieved this, but I will venture two suggestions: 1) he has purposely required us to believe things that society deems foolish; and 2) he has made the Bible something that can easily be understood at a superficial level, but that cannot be more fully understood without time and humility. I'll explain what I mean about each of these ploys below.

The Bible requires you to believe things that high society would consider foolish

I personally believe some outlandish things. I believe that a donkey spoke to Balaam, as is recounted in the book of Numbers. I believe that Jonah was swallowed by a whale and was regurgitated up on land near Nineveh three days later, alive. I believe that all the animals on the earth today are descended from a smallish group of animals that fled into Noah's ark before God flooded the whole earth. When I have mentioned these beliefs to people who think of themselves as intelligent, their immediate reaction has been one of disbelief that I could believe such nonsense. (I recounted my own similar reaction in chapter 1 when I met with evangelicals who believed in a literal six-day creation.)

I know of people who became Christians by means of what might seem to be a logical order of events: first they became sceptical of the theory of evolution; then they got convinced of the truth of the Bible's creation account; and finally they chose to believe the rest of the Bible, including the Gospel of salvation from hell through faith in Christ. However, this logical and deductive progression isn't how most people become Christians. My own conversion is more standard. First I became aware of my own sinfulness;[8] then I became

---

[8] The major means that the Lord used for this was in fact the words of my non-Christian brother, who said that he could count on the fingers of one hand the people in Serbia who had been willing to stand up to Milošević's rule there (my brother was a war reporter in Yugoslavia at the time). I began to question whether I would have been one of them if a similar thing happened in England, and

aware through the witness of Christians, and reading the Bible, that my sins could be forgiven; and finally I reached out for that forgiveness, and have clung tightly to it ever since. Without Christ's forgiveness I would be in a terrible mess, both now and at the point of my death.

On my conversion, I experienced something I had never experienced before: the reality of communication with the living God. Yes, I had prayed many times over the years before my conversion, but it was a lifeless affair— sometimes my prayers just involved reciting a memorised prayer (e.g. what gets called The Lord's Prayer). What a lifeless way to communicate with someone! Imagine if a friend of yours always mumbled speedily the very same few sentences to you. It would be a sure-fire way to make you want to avoid that person.

Other prayers I made before my conversion were more genuine, but I hadn't yet got right with God (i.e. sought his forgiveness), so they were generally met with silence. After my conversion, however, my prayer life became part of a real relationship with the living God. Of course, this claim will be seen as delusional by the people who see the belief that a donkey spoke as foolish. However, I have experienced genuine communion with God, as have millions of others like me. And if you know something to be true, it makes little difference how many people mock you for it.

Soon after my conversion I heard a sermon by an elder at my church in which he mentioned that the Bible makes it clear that the world was made by God in six days. By that

---

similarly, whether I would have done likewise if I had lived in Nazi Germany. After much soul-searching I concluded that I simply couldn't trust myself to have behaved so honourably. Far from it.

stage I had no trouble at all believing that. I personally knew the God of creation, and knew that he was capable of anything at all.

In terms of my own conversion, then, the order of events was as follows: first I was forgiven; then I began a relationship with God; then I learnt that he is reliable; and now I believe every word in the Bible. As a result, I believe things that the intelligentsia consider foolish—things that *I also* considered foolish before my conversion—which brings us to the main point. The fact that the Bible is full of seemingly unbelievable stories is off-putting to people who have a high view of themselves. It gives the Bible an air of disreputability. It means you have to swallow your pride in order to accept its teaching. It means you'll look foolish to your friends and peers. Yet those who are already near the bottom of the pile have far less to lose than those who are considered big shots (or consider themselves to be big shots). And so the humble are far more likely than the proud to believe these stories, and with them, the Bible's message as a whole.

If it was necessary to be very clever to believe the Bible, it would attract many more proud people. But, in reality, the Bible's core message is very simple to understand—I am sinful; I need forgiveness; and Jesus offers me forgiveness through his work on the cross. The kind of people who view their own intellect very highly will not want to be seen to believe such things if doing so would require them also to believe a story about a talking donkey. The following passage, which comes from the first letter Paul wrote to the church in Corinth, sums the situation up very nicely:

'For the word of the cross is folly to those who are perishing, but to us who are being saved it is the power of God. For it is written,

"I will destroy the wisdom of the wise, and the discernment of the discerning I will thwart."

Where is the one who is wise? Where is the scribe? Where is the debater of this age? Has not God made foolish the wisdom of the world? For since, in the wisdom of God, the world did not know God through wisdom, it pleased God through the folly of what we preach to save those who believe. For Jews demand signs and Greeks seek wisdom, but we preach Christ crucified, a stumbling block to Jews and folly to Gentiles, but to those who are called, both Jews and Greeks, Christ the power of God and the wisdom of God. For the foolishness of God is wiser than men, and the weakness of God is stronger than men.' (1 Cor 1:18-25)

God has shown incredible wisdom in making the message of the Bible something that appeals to the humble, but not to the proud, and including seemingly unbelievable events in its text is one way that he has done so. Below I will propose another way in which he has done so.

The Bible can easily be understood at a superficial level, but requires humility for a deeper understanding

I have personally experienced strikingly different levels of success when it comes to learning new things. At school, things came easily to me. I tended to be near the top of the year throughout the majority of my school years in almost every subject. I imagine that the ease at which I learnt things, and the minimal effort I needed to put in to perform well, was a frustration to some of my fellow students to whom things didn't come so easily. I was not particularly gracious about this, but instead was rather proud of my achievements.

By my late teenage years, I was in a rather different position. Through arrogantly disregarding my doctors' and parents' advice, I felt that I was only going to benefit from taking illegal drugs. The opposite was the case. What little benefit I got from my drug taking was drowned out by fairly major mental health problems.

To cut a long story short, I then found myself starting a university career in a very different state of mind to that which I had spent most of my schooling. I was taking heavy sedatives, and found basic tasks such as reading and even deep thinking to be virtually impossible. I failed my first year, and then changed to study a course that involved virtually no reading—maths. With a lot of help from my older brother, I did manage to get a degree. Just. Afterwards I got a graduate job, and started work with an intake of seventeen other people. Of the eighteen of us, I was the one who most struggled to learn what was necessary for the job. I was still taking heavy sedatives, and I found it very hard to pick up the new concepts that we were learning. I was not a Christian at this point, and, although I had stopped taking illegal drugs, I still drank a lot of alcohol, which didn't go well with my medication.

By God's grace, about two years after starting that job I became a Christian. I still take medication, but thankfully I manage myself much better—getting all the sleep I need and avoiding alcohol altogether—and so I have become a good and successful worker. However, I am still much slower at picking things up than when I was a schoolboy, and I have to work very hard to succeed.

With my personal history I know fully what it is like to pick things up easily and quickly, and to be proud with it. I also know how hard it can be to learn new things, and that patience and hard work are often necessary for me to grasp new concepts and ideas. In reality, the second of these two ways of learning has tended to achieve a much deeper level of learning than did the first, in which I often had a quick superficial understanding, but no real depth. And, interestingly, the way the Bible needs to be studied is much more like this second way of learning. It is written in such a way that patience, hard work, and the willingness to be teachable are necessary to get a deeper understanding of it. Yes, you can acquire a superficial knowledge of the Bible quite quickly. And for many people, this superficial level is all they want. Over the years, I have spoken to hundreds of people who are convinced that they know the Bible well. Yet they only in fact have a superficial knowledge of it, which soon becomes very apparent. Nevertheless, they boast about their knowledge of the Bible. I would have been the same in my school days. Things came easily to me, and I had a confidence that I could fully understand things without needing to study hard.

There are so many levels to the text of the Bible that no-one is able to pick up all the key messages in a short space of time. I have read the Bible every day for over twenty years, but many people have spent their entire lives studying the Bible, and neither I nor they have got close to understanding it in its fullness.

An example of the many levels at which the Bible is written is the well-known parable in Luke 15, often called the Prodigal Son, in which a son takes his inheritance early, leaves his family home, and squanders his money on loose living. He eventually decides to return home, however, at which point his father welcomes him with outstretched arms.

I initially took this parable to mean that God is willing to forgive even those of us who have been very sinful, and done what we know to be wrong, which was a useful understanding of it for someone like me.

Many years later though, I became more aware of the second son in the story, who had stayed at home with his father. He resented the father's forgiveness and generosity towards his younger brother. I also became aware of the fact that this parable came just after two others about lost things—a lost coin and a lost sheep. It became clear to me that the parable of the prodigal son would be better called the parable of the two lost sons. Just like the sheep and the coin, one brother was away from home, and knew that he was lost (like the sheep), but the other was lost at home, and didn't know that he was lost (like the coin). The younger son was lost through his own sin, the elder brother through his self-righteousness. This was a new understanding that I had learnt.

And there was still much more to learn. I have recently come to appreciate that in the parables of the lost coin and the lost sheep a search was made for the lost items. Only in the case of the prodigal son was there no search for the thing that was lost. It was the elder son's duty to search for his younger brother, and yet he didn't.

The chapter begins by telling us that both the sinful ('the tax collectors and sinners'), and the self-righteous ('the Pharisees and scribes'), were present for Jesus' parables. Consequently, the parables serve as a criticism of the assembled Pharisees and scribes for not having done their duty—for not having gone out looking to bring the sinners back into the fold. They also serve to speak of the true elder brother—Christ himself, who 'came to seek and save the lost' (Luke 19:10).

Rather, then, than coming to a quick superficial understanding of the passage, I have learned much more from Luke 15 than I did with my original reading. I have achieved this by being patient, by being humble enough to keep reading it, and by being willing to learn from others. The Bible rewards the humble, patient reader.

As I say, if all you want to do is quickly read the Bible, then you can get some sense of what it says, but not a terribly deep sense. For example, I have often heard people talk about the fact that in Leviticus homosexuality and the eating of shellfish are alike described as an abomination to God. These people then suggest that Christians should spend more of their time concentrating on the 'sin' of eating shellfish, and less on the sin of homosexuality. However, this is a very basic reading of the Bible. Below I'll try to give a fuller and better explanation - the kind that you can only develop over time, with patient study.

Many people know that a new covenant (or testament) was introduced by Christ. This new covenant contains the rules by which Christians should live. They need to live by *those* laws rather than the covenant that was given to the nation of Israel through Moses. And just as there are similarities and differences between the legal systems of different countries (e.g. murder is wrong in both Germany and the UK, but jay-walking is only illegal in Germany), there are similarities and differences between the different Biblical testaments. And, notably, homosexual behaviour is prohibited in both.[9] Eating kosher, however, is an Old-Testament-only law. The Jews ate different food because they were to be a physically distinct group of people. Hence, in addition to their food laws, they were given many laws about how they were to look and what they were to wear.

So, there are areas where the Old Testament is similar to the New Testament, but there are also areas where it is different. Keeping kosher is only necessary in one, while sexual purity is required in both.

That the New Testament has different laws to the Old Testament is quite a basic concept, so if people overlook it, it is likely that, through a lack of humility, they have rushed to a quick conclusion, perhaps to satisfy a particular agenda.

In sum, then, the Bible appeals to the humble: it can be understood at a superficial level, but it only reveals its full treasures to those who approach it with humility. I'm sure there are many other ways in which God has made the Bible's message appeal to the humble rather than the proud, but the examples above should suffice for now.

---

[9] Please note, homosexual sex is just one of a multitude of things prohibited in the New Testament, including a whole variety of other sexual sins. (In fact, as we saw in the Sermon on the Mount in chapter 3, even lustful desires, let alone acting them out, are sinful in the New Testament.) All have sinned, whether gay or straight – homosexual sexual sins are no more sinful than heterosexual sexual sins.

SIX

Its Style is Unusually Truthful and Modest

Small children often tell outlandish stories. They think they are fooling their listeners, but most adults know when a child is making things up. There are tell-tale signs—small children haven't learned what is feasible and what isn't, and so their claims are often outlandish, and easy to spot. The schoolteacher knows full well that dogs rarely eat homework.

But children aren't the only ones who embellish the truth. Adults also often do so. I remember interviewing a candidate for a job who made totally unrealistic claims about her past work. Having worked in the industry myself, I was able to spot them. I pointed this out to my fellow interview panellists, and yet, remarkably, they viewed the candidate's lies as a positive! It showed initiative, or so they thought. I didn't feel the same way myself.

Since becoming a Christian, I have had far less success in interviews. I can no longer just lie to an interviewer, so if I'm asked a question about things I have no experience of, I have to say so. By God's grace, though, I have been successful in a few interviews. But I'm certainly fighting an uphill battle.

83

The fact that people lie in interviews is important to consider in this chapter. People very rarely lie to make themselves look worse. The goal in lying is to make yourself look better.

However, much of the Bible is written in a way that makes its key characters look worse than they might have chosen themselves (if they felt at liberty to lie). The main characters are presented 'warts and all'. We're told that Moses and David—two of the most prominent men of God in the Old Testament's narrative—were murderers. And Peter and Paul aren't given an easy ride by the New Testament's writers either. They tell us that Peter disowned his Lord Jesus when he most needed support, and that Paul rounded up Christians in order to put them to death.

These are hardly the kind of things you would want to publicise about key figures in a movement that you were trying to sell to outsiders. But if you're committed to portraying events as they actually occurred, whether good or bad, then these are the kind of things that have to be included.

Granted, critical writing is common in some contexts,[10] but at the time of the Bible's composition, it was not the norm. For example, notice how boastful this 9th century BC text of the Phoenician king Kilamuwa is:

> 'I am Kilamuwa, the son of King [some missing text]. King Gabar reigned over Ya'diya but

---

[10] I say 'in some contexts', because it often depends on who is being written about, and who is doing the writing. Compare for example the different portrayals that Fox News and CNN gave of the two candidates for the 2020 US presidential election. They were each either gushing in praise or hyper-critical, depending on who they were talking about.

achieved nothing. Then came Bamah, and he achieved nothing. My own father, Haya', did nothing with his reign. My brother, Sha'il, also did nothing. It was I, Kilamuwa ... who managed to do what none of my ancestors had.'[11]

Compare that to a very typical passage from the Bible about an Israelite king:

> 'Ahaziah the son of Ahab began to reign over Israel in Samaria in the seventeenth year of Jehoshaphat king of Judah, and he reigned for two years over Israel. He did what was evil in the sight of the LORD and walked in the way of his father and in the way of his mother and in the way of Jeroboam the son of Nebat, who made Israel to sin.' (1 Kings 22:51-52)

Such statements are commonplace in the historical books of the Old Testament—the characters aren't smartened up. As the Bible scholar, Dr Peter Williams says, 'Amenhotep from Egypt tells you Amenhotep was great; Ramses from Egypt tells you Ramses is great; Kilamuwa, the Phoenician king, tells you Kilamuwa is great. That's what they do. One thing we can say about the books of Kings in the Old Testament [is that] they are not written as royal propaganda. They just don't have that pattern at all.'[12]

---

[11] As cited in *The Reliability of the Old Testament - Dr. Peter J. Williams* (2020) <https://www.youtube.com/watch?v=qEgxTkTu4Ig> accessed 29 May 2023.
[12] ibid.

The Bible has been written in a very self-critical style, which makes it stand alone when compared to other writings of its time.

Another way that the Bible demonstrates an unusual honesty is in its literary style, particularly in the case of historical narratives. The Biblical text often describes remarkable events, and yet does so with very modest language. Had we written the Bible, we'd probably use more extravagant language. Just think about the kind of language often used to promote films: 'spell-binding', 'stunning', 'a must see', etc. However, the Bible's authors use very matter-of-fact and often understatedly brief text.

Mel Gibson famously made a film called *The Passion of the Christ* in which he endeavoured to portray the gruesomeness of crucifixion. He devoted a great deal of the film's running time to what the Apostle John succinctly and simply wrote as follows:

> 'So they took Jesus, and he went out, bearing his own cross, to the place called The Place of a Skull, which in Aramaic is called Golgotha. There they crucified him, and with him two others, one on either side, and Jesus between them.' (John 19:16-18)

John clearly felt no need to use elaborate language. He simply stated the facts. The event in question was so great in and of itself that it didn't need a Hollywood-style makeover.

As for the miraculous, consider these two passages:

'Then he ordered the crowds to sit down on the grass, and taking the five loaves and the two fish, he looked up to heaven and said a blessing. Then he broke the loaves and gave them to the disciples, and the disciples gave them to the crowds. And they all ate and were satisfied. And they took up twelve baskets full of the broken pieces left over. And those who ate were about five thousand men, besides women and children.' (Matthew 14:19-21)

'While he was still speaking, someone from the ruler's house came and said, "Your daughter is dead; do not trouble the Teacher any more." But Jesus on hearing this answered him, "Do not fear; only believe, and she will be well." And when he came to the house, he allowed no one to enter with him, except Peter and John and James, and the father and mother of the child. And all were weeping and mourning for her, but he said, "Do not weep, for she is not dead but sleeping." And they laughed at him, knowing that she was dead. But taking her by the hand he called, saying, "Child, arise." And her spirit returned, and she got up at once. And he directed that something should be given her to eat. And her parents were amazed, but he charged them to tell no one what had happened.' (Luke 8:49-56)

These miracles are written with an understatement which is consistent with Jesus' own desire to keep the latter miracle quiet. Jesus came with a message that spoke for itself. Miracles were a natural part of having the Son of God walk

on the earth; it was his message and his work on the cross that really did the talking.

The Bible, then, is a book that portrays its events with unusual honesty. And that honesty reveals that the authors had a confidence that the message was true. As a result, it needed no embellishment. There is no need to boast when you're confident of the truth of what you are saying. Conversely, when you're not, you use extravagant language to make your message seem more impressive, like the small children we thought about at the start of this chapter.

88

SEVEN

It is Studyable for Life

Many millions of people read the Bible every single day. They don't read it because they think that it is magic, and that the mere act of reading it will give them a special blessing (as certain adherents of other religions do, who even read their sacred texts in languages they can't understand). Instead, Christians read the Bible, and in fact study it hard, because they think that understanding it will make them better people, give them guidance for life, and most importantly, help them to know their God better.

I personally studied English literature for A-level (i.e. to age 18), and so I studied a number of books in reasonable depth. I have also read many books that I have not formally studied. Some works of literature have a huge amount of depth to them—for instance, the writings of George Orwell and John Steinbeck had a significant impact on me. However, aside from the Bible, I cannot think of another book that I would be able to study every single day of my adult life, and yet continue to learn new things about. No matter how much I enjoyed Orwell's *1984*, and its relevance to today, I simply couldn't study it in depth every day. I would run out of things to study and learn from it. Not so with the Bible.

I remember once discussing with my housemate, James, what he would do differently in life if he came to the conclusion that the Christian faith wasn't true. He said that for a start he would stop reading the Bible. This brought me to the verge of tears. I study the Bible more intensely than the vast majority of the world, but I don't come close to the sheer time and effort he puts into studying it. He spends hours every day studying it. As a result, he has many people who are interested in reading the fruits of his study. I was desperately sad to think of the possibility of him stopping reading it altogether.

And James doesn't himself come close to the intensity with which some people throughout history have studied the Bible, and the length of time for which they have studied it. He is only in his forties. I have known many people who have studied the Bible every day for many more years than he, or I, have been alive.

So how can so many people never tire of intensely studying a single book? Well, the Bible is no ordinary book. For a start, it is in fact a collection of 66 books, covering a whole array of writing styles.

Some books are largely historical accounts of events, such as the books of Kings.

Others are prophetic in nature, i.e. speaking of the future. Their writing style is very different to that of historical narratives.

Some writing is called wisdom literature, e.g. the book of Proverbs. As with modern English proverbs, such as 'many hands make light work', Biblical proverbs have an underlying truth, but they won't hold true in each and every circumstance. (Sometimes 'too many cooks spoil the broth'.) So, this is another completely different writing style to study.

The New Testament contains many letters, written by one person to another person or to a group of people. They sometimes, therefore, contain very personal touches, since the writer intimately knows who he is writing to. At the same time, they come closest to what could be described as a manual of instructions for a believer. The Church was in its infancy when these letters were being written, and very often Paul was having to explain correct doctrine to his readers. As a result, Paul's letters tend to be quite systematic, involving thorough explanations of how we are to behave and why. So, this is another completely different style of writing to have to study.

The Book of Psalms is a book of song lyrics. As is the case with many modern songs, the Psalms are very emotional. There are psalms of love, frustration, sadness, despair, happiness, worship, joy. And these emotions are often conveyed by poetic devices. One such device is the use of acrostic writing, which makes every line start with a different letter of the Hebrew alphabet, so each letter of the alphabet starts one and only one of the psalm's lines.

The Psalms' use of acrostic structures is significant. Every letter of the alphabet needs to be exploited to do justice to the Psalms' subject matter. In a similar way, we need to read every style of Biblical writing to get the fullest understanding of its message.

As readers, we have preferred writing styles. I particularly enjoy the narratives of the Gospels. They are accounts of real events, and real things that were said, but each Gospel writer arranges his Gospel differently in order to emphasise different points. I love to try and understand what those points are, since they don't necessarily come across from a cursory reading.

Many Christians prefer reading the letters of Paul, which, as I said above, are the closest writing style we have in the Bible to a straightforward manual on Christian living. And almost all Christians love the Psalms, full of heartfelt emotion. However, the acrostic psalms teach us to read the whole array of Biblical literature, not just the styles of writing that most appeal to us, which makes the Bible a book that can be studied every day of one's life.

In addition to the many writing styles within it, the Bible is written in such a way that it is impossible to understand fully at first reading. True, some things can be understood straightaway, but many things take a lot more time. For example, there are apparent discrepancies or contradictions within the text. Now, some people are very keen to consider the Bible to be wrong, and so when they encounter what *appears* to be an error in the text, they quickly decide that it is indeed an error. They then cast the Bible off as unreliable. But that is too hasty an approach. Deep study of the Bible as a whole can often illuminate something that at first glance looks to be problematic.

Some of these 'errors' concern the Bible's factual content. For many years, critics rubbished the Bible's account of the people group, the Hittites, due to the lack of archaeological evidence for them. That was until archaeological evidence was indeed found in the 19th century, which supported what the Bible said. Now there is a wealth of evidence for this people group. The Bible had been right all along. (Had the Bible's critics been more patient, they would not have ended up embarrassed.)

Of course, the normal reader of the Bible is not an archaeologist and doesn't, therefore, have the tools at his disposal to compare the Bible with the relevant external evidence. But the normal reader *is* able to trust what he reads, and the principle of being willing to trust the Bible and its words is a very important one. As I said above, many people are too quick to decide that the Bible is wrong on the basis of apparent errors within its text. But the Bible's 'errors' are there by design. And if the reader, rather than quickly rubbishing the text of scripture, tries to understand what the Bible has done, then he will, after much study, be able to do just that.

A nice example are Luke and Matthew's much maligned accounts of Judas's death. As many sceptics have pointed out, these accounts of Judas's death contain discrepancies, yet, with much study, those discrepancies have been wonderfully explained by my housemate, James. I say wonderfully, because the very fact that there were seeming discrepancies in the two accounts has allowed him to see things in the text of scripture that he wouldn't otherwise have seen. As he says himself, 'Tension in the Biblical narrative doesn't exist to be reconciled away; it exists to make us think more carefully about Scripture's detail, complexity, and beauty.'

It goes beyond the scope of this book to detail fully James's account of the differences between the two accounts of

Judas's death, but please do read his paper[13] if you would like an explanation. (You can find other papers on his Academia site that cover other well-known discrepancies in the Bible.)

The lesson to learn is thus as follows: the Bible is written in such a way that it rewards careful and diligent study. People who want to rubbish the Bible will soon find plenty of things to rubbish, and so if you don't want to study the Bible in depth, you can quickly justify your decision to toss it out completely. I have often encountered people who choose to do just this, and perhaps you have too—people with a very limited knowledge of the Bible who nevertheless loudly proclaim they have found errors in it. But as I discussed in chapter 5, the Bible is written in a way to appeal to the humble, and not to the proud. After all, it involves humility to admit that you don't understand the seeming discrepancies in the Bible, and then to set about studying hard until you do.

The Bible thus rewards its diligent and humble students. This is because it has been supernaturally written so that it encourages deep study. But, even with in-depth daily study for an entire lifetime, the student of the Bible will never exhaust what can be learnt.

---

[13] James Bejon, 'The Death of Judas in Matthew & Luke-Acts' <https://www.academia.edu/40801768> accessed 29 January 2022.

EIGHT

It Changes Lives

My final proof that the Bible is worth reading is simply that it changes lives. An atheist arrived on a South Pacific island (so the story goes) to find lots of local people reading the Bible. He spoke to one of them, saying, 'You don't believe that book do you? We all now know that it's not true.' In response, the man simply said, 'Sir, if I didn't believe this book, you would be inside my belly right now!'

The Bible is a book that changes lives. Many South Pacific islands had a history of cannibalism, but through the work of Christian evangelists bringing the Bible to those lands, they have largely been converted into strong Christian communities, and in the process, cannibalism has disappeared.

Imagine you were walking alone down a dark street one night and you saw a dozen young men walking towards you. You might feel slightly intimidated. Would seeing a Bible under each of their arms settle any fears you might have for your safety? I venture it would. Even the most ardent anti-Christian would probably have to admit as much.

Not everyone likes the *message* of the Bible, but very few people would expect a group of Bible-carrying Christians to be much of a physical threat. Now, I appreciate that historically Catholics, for example, have engaged in a fair bit of violence, but it would be rare to see a group of Catholics all carrying Bibles. It is, after all, specifically reading the Bible that changes lives, which Catholics rarely do.

It is worth pausing here to refute an oft-trotted-out meme. I have had many people tell me over the years that religion is the cause of most wars. This is simply not true. If we just look at the wars of the last century, we can easily see that neither of the biggest wars—the First and Second World Wars—were wars about religion. Nor were the Vietnam and Korean wars. At a push you could say that the wars of independence in Yugoslavia had a religious *element*, but there were many other factors in play, and the same is true of Afghanistan and Iraq.

So to blithely state, as I have heard many people do, that all wars stem from religion is patently not true. And even if there is an element of truth to it, religion is not an especially specific term. I personally have no real desire to defend the activities of Muslims, Hindus or Catholics, for example. Not all religions, after all, are the same. As we saw in chapter 4 the Bible has a very different message to all other religions. True, many other religions have similarities with Biblical Christianity, but of course, forgeries are only believable if they look like the real thing in some way. No-one would believe that a Monopoly £50 note was a real bank note, but if I paid for my shopping with a good forgery of a £50 note, only the most discerning shop worker could tell that it wasn't real.

So, even if 'religion' was a contributory factor to a reasonably large proportion of wars (which I question anyway), Bible-believing Christianity wouldn't normally be the culprit. More likely, it would be religions that claim to be Christian, but whose members are very rarely encouraged to actually read the Bible and let it govern how they live. As I said in chapter 1, there are religious types who claim to be Christians, but who don't let the Bible influence their lives. Such people are largely indistinguishable from other people—they lie and lust, and put themselves and their own family first—just like most other people. However, Biblical Christianity—i.e. a faith rooted in regular humble study of the Bible—changes lives.

Biblical Christians are thus quite different from the rest of the world, and quite different from how they themselves were prior to their conversion.

For example, I believe wholeheartedly that I deserve hell for my many sins. That is quite an unusual thing for a religious person to believe. Most religious people hope that they have done enough good things to enter heaven. Not so a Biblical Christian. As a Bible-believing Christian, I am certain that if God judged me for how I have led my life, I would end up in hell. Nevertheless, I also believe that I will definitely go to heaven, because Christ has paid my entrance fee (as it were) by bearing the punishment that I deserve. I never used to think this way until I started reading the Bible.

So, reading and believing the Bible changes the way people think. And it also changes the way they act. I was a heavy drug taker and drinker in my pre-conversion days. I was also very self-centred, always putting myself first. I'm now a clean-living individual, who is very happy to put other

people's interests ahead of my own (not as much as I should, but certainly a great deal more than I did before my conversion). Of course, you may not be a wild-living selfish person. The only point I am making now is that believing the Bible had a big impact on me. Like the former cannibal, my life has been drastically changed by believing the Bible. And many Bible-believing Christians can testify to the very same life-changing effect.

Take, for example, the 18th century slave trader, John Newton. After his conversion, as well as penning the much-loved hymn, Amazing Grace, Newton became very active in the abolitionist movement alongside politicians like William Wilberforce. This movement ultimately brought an end to the slave trade in the British Empire. What a turnaround! What a changed life! And yet, Newton would never have considered himself to be a good person. Rather, he said in that famous hymn that he considered it to be a work of 'amazing grace…that saved *a wretch* like me'. His life was radically changed for the better—he was a much-improved human being—and even then he still considered himself to be totally unworthy of heaven without God's grace.

Throughout the centuries, countless lives have been drastically changed by believing the Bible. I hope that by now you think that it is worth reading the Bible for yourself. If you do, and let it do its work, it will change you too.

The last chapter will discuss some pointers about how to read the Bible for yourself.

NINE

How to Go About Reading it Yourself

My hope, if you have got this far, is that you will now want to read the Bible for yourself. As we've already noted, however, the Bible isn't an ordinary book, and so it can't easily be read like any other book, i.e. from start to finish in one go. As a result, you might need some guidance as to how to best read it. And that's what I'll try to give in this chapter. But please don't take my guidance as the only way to read the Bible. And please do feel free to develop your own approach. So long as you do actually read it. Whatever causes you to read it rather than let it gather dust on your shelves is a good thing.

Probably the first thing you should do is choose a translation to read (assuming you don't read the languages it was originally written in: Hebrew, Greek and Aramaic). Translations tend to sit within a spectrum of being very close to the original languages at one end (literal translations) and being more readable at the other end. Hebrew word order, for example, is different from English word order, and Greek idioms are different from English idioms. So, to make the English more readable and understandable, translators have to steer away from word for word translations.

When I first started reading the Bible, I chose a Bible based on its size (perhaps not the most important reason for choosing a Bible). I wanted a small, pocket Bible, and the smallest one I could find happened to be the New American Standard Bible. This is quite a literal translation, and as a result, I wouldn't describe it as especially easy to read. At the other end of the spectrum are translations like the Good News Bible, which is very easy to read (and is aimed at younger or unconfident readers). The important thing is to choose a translation that you're comfortable with. I personally read the English Standard Version as my main translation (but I often look at other translations as well, just to get a sense of what different translators make of certain passages). I find it quite literal (so I get a good sense of the original languages), but also very comfortable for me to read. I would encourage you to try to read more literal translations if you can, but if you find them too hard-going, do feel free to read more easy-to-read translations like the Good News Bible or the slightly more literal New International Version.

Most translations are fine, so don't worry too much about whether you have chosen 'the right one'. That said, I would warn against a few translations. I would personally not recommend reading the King James Bible. Its old English is a hindrance, and you don't gain anything by reading the Bible in archaic language. I would also strongly discourage reading the Message and the Passion translations, which are the works of individual translators who have put their own agendas onto their translations. Similarly, I would avoid the Jehovah's Witnesses' Watchtower Bible, which, like the Message and the Passion, changes the translation to suit the translators' theology, rather than letting the Bible speak freely.

So how to read it?

If you start reading at page 1, you should happily be able to read the whole of Genesis (perhaps skipping through the occasional list of names), and the first twenty chapters of Exodus, but before long you will get bogged down in the intricacies of the laws given to the nation of Israel in the rest of the Pentateuch (that's the name given to the first five books in the Bible—Genesis, Exodus, Leviticus, Numbers and Deuteronomy). You might then put the Bible down, not to pick it up again, which would be a terrible shame. So, to avoid that outcome, I would recommend the following approach.

Read the New Testament a lot, at least initially. The Gospels, Acts and the letters of the New Testament all have a lot of low-hanging fruit. What I mean by that is that it's easy to glean nuggets of wisdom and truth from them without much effort. Also read the more historical books of the Old Testament (books like Joshua, Judges through to Ezra and Nehemiah). They have easy-to-understand stories in them, which makes them easy to read. In addition, they provide a historical backdrop for the other books of the Old Testament. You'll soon begin to understand why the writings of the prophets (Isaiah through to Malachi) keep coming back to the failings of the people of Israel.

Don't read the Bible like this forever though. Children have an immediate liking for meat, potatoes and dessert without much coaxing from their parents, but over time, by gradually introducing things like broccoli and spinach into meals,

children can develop a taste for a well-balanced diet. So it is with scripture. Some books, like the books of Chronicles, have long streams of names of people, called genealogies. Feel free initially to skip those lists of names. There will come a time when you will crave the 'spinach' of genealogies, but it will take a lot of Bible reading first, and it's not a good idea to force yourself to read things that might lead you to give up reading altogether.

Do, however, set yourself goals of reading less-instantly-gratifying books. One way to read the harder-to-read books is to read them in tandem with easier-to-read books. So, perhaps you could read through the long and somewhat heavy-going book of Jeremiah, whilst at the same time reading through a Gospel. (Read a bit of both books every day.) And if you're finding a particular book too arduous, don't feel bad if you want to stop reading it and instead move on to an easier-to-read book. Your ability to read the harder books will come with time. Remember, though, that while the goal is to read all of scripture, Rome wasn't built in a day. I'm hoping you'll read the Bible for the rest of your life. There is plenty of time to become more expert in the laws in Leviticus.

Here are some general tips on reading different writing styles in the Bible.

The letters

Some books really benefit from being read through in one sitting. Into that camp go the New Testament letters. If you received a letter from a friend, you'd likely read it all in one go. That way you'd get the whole message straight away. I would recommend trying to make it a goal to do the same thing with the letters in the New Testament. Then, having read them through, go back and read them more slowly, perhaps just a chapter at a time. True, some letters are quite long, and reading them through in one go can be a bit intimidating. You don't *have* to read them that way. But you could start by reading some of the shorter letters all the way through.

Also, bear in mind that the letters in the Bible have all been written with a purpose. The writers aren't just killing some time by writing to a friend. There was often a particular reason (or more than one) why the writer wrote to specific people at specific times. See if you can work out what that was. And then bring that understanding to the whole letter. Remember, you are reading a letter that wasn't addressed to you. Perhaps not all of it is as relevant to you as it was to the original recipients. Try and work out what in the letters counts for all Christians, and what is specific to the audience for which it was written.

Also, ask questions about scripture, e.g. 'Why is he saying that?', 'Why to them?'. However, and this is important, bear in mind that you won't be able to answer every question you ask—at least not straight away. As we discussed in chapter 7, many people quickly reject the Bible when they read things that don't instantly make sense to them, or can't instantly be explained. I would strongly encourage you to hang such things on a peg in your mind, to come back to at a later date. No-one knows everything about the Bible. No-one at all. Watch out for people who think they do. It is absolutely fine to not understand something, or even to think that something seems contradictory in the Bible. Just leave it hanging like that, and move on. At some point in the

future, you will start to tie up the loose ends. You've got the whole of the rest of your life to do that, and beyond!

The Gospels

The other main writings in the New Testament are the Gospels—Matthew, Mark, Luke and John. There is a lot that can be easily understood in the Gospels. But the more you read them, more questions will arise. One thing I encourage you to do with the Gospels is to treat them as individual books, i.e. not to spend too long trying to harmonise them all into one account. I appreciate that there's some benefit in harmonisation, but at the end of the day they were each written as standalone books. Each Gospel writer has different things he wants to emphasise about Jesus' life.

Ask yourself questions about the flow of the events. 'Why does this section come before that section and after this other section? What is being emphasised in the flow of events?' Different Gospel writers put things in different orders to emphasise different things. Other good questions to ask are 'Why does this word keep getting repeated? What is its significance? What is being emphasised?'

In general, ask questions of the text. It will stand up to scrutiny. You may not get answers straight away, but eventually they will come.

Other narratives

One of the unique things about the Gospels is that they tell the story of someone who led a perfect life—Jesus. The rest of the Biblical narrative doesn't, so you need to work out whether or not what is said or done by different characters in the Biblical narrative is in line with God's desires.

As we saw in chapter 6, the Bible recounts both the positive things that its characters say and do as well as the negative things. The book of Job, for example, is basically one long conversation between five people. Some of what they each say falls in line with God's will, and some is opposed to it.

Over time, by reading the whole of scripture more and more, it will become easier to determine when its characters are speaking and behaving in line with God's desires, and when they aren't. So, fully understanding Job will take many years of experience of reading scripture. And yet, the basic principles of the book can be understood relatively easily. This is a common theme to studying scripture: as we saw in chapter 5 it can be understood at many levels, and it takes humility to admit that you, as a reader, will always be learning from it.

Prophecy

One key style of writing in scripture is prophecy. It is often not straightforward in the Old Testament prophetic books to know who is speaking at a given time in the text. Furthermore, the identity of the speaker often changes. Is it God? Is it the prophet himself? Is the prophet speaking on behalf of the people? These are good questions to ask of any passage of Old Testament prophecy. Also, Old Testament prophets tend to foresee three main future timeframes: the near future of the people to whom the prophet is speaking (usually the Israelites); the first coming of Christ (1st century AD); and the second coming of Christ (still future). The nature of prophetic writing is to sometimes move between those three timeframes quite swiftly.

New Testament prophecy likewise concentrates on three timeframes, but they are different to the Old Testament timeframes. A lot of New Testament prophetic writing points towards the impending judgment of Israel and the destruction of Jerusalem and its temple in AD 70; a lot points towards the time at the very end of the present age, when Christ will return; and the third timeframe is the Church age, i.e. the whole sweep of history from Christ's ascension into heaven until he returns to earth.

Some Christians try to make all New Testament prophecy fit into only one of these timeframes, but you will have a more fruitful understanding of New Testament prophecy if you allow it to cover all three. Meanwhile, the more you gain an appreciation of Old Testament prophecy, the more you will understand New Testament prophecy—there is a huge amount of overlap between the two. And, as always, remember, if you don't understand something, just mentally put it to one side and return to it at a later date.

The Psalms

I would encourage reading the Psalms regularly, i.e. alongside other books. That said, there have been times in my Christian life when I have been so low and defeated by circumstances that I couldn't read any books of the Bible apart from the Psalms. And even then, I often couldn't read many of the more positive psalms. There are many psalms of despair—Psalm 88 is perhaps the bleakest—and sometimes reading them is exactly what you need. At the same time, there are many other types of psalms. I would recommend reading them regularly to appreciate the full range of emotions that the Christian life can involve.

The Law

The first five books of the Bible are collectively known as the Law of Moses (or the Pentateuch). The first of the five, Genesis, is mainly a historical narrative, while the next four books are more legal in nature: they contain the laws God prescribed for the newly-formed nation of Israel. As we discussed in chapter 5, Christians are not under the jurisdiction of this Law. It was intended to govern the nation of Israel. As you read the Law of Moses, try to think about which laws relate just to Israel. (This will come with time by learning which laws Christians in the New Testament are expected to keep, and which they aren't.) In addition, ask yourself why that nation needed such laws, and why we might not need them now as New Testament believers.

At the same time, bear in mind that the Law of Moses tells us a lot about the nature of the God who gave it. See whether you can see his character in the individual laws. Many of the laws also prefigure Christ in some way. We saw in chapter 2, in our study of typology, that certain *people* prefigure Jesus (we looked at Joseph, Moses and Isaac). Some of the very laws in the Law of Moses, including the whole sacrificial system detailed within it, likewise prefigure Christ. See whether you can spot these foreshadows of Christ inside the Law of Moses.

The Proverbs

The book of Proverbs, as the name suggests, is full of short and wise proverbs. I don't think it is intended to be read from start to finish. Normally it is important to consider the context within which Bible verses appear. This is less important with the Proverbs. Conveniently, there are 31 chapters in the book of Proverbs. So if you want to read a bit of Proverbs one day, choose the chapter number that matches the day of the month that it is, and read that chapter. Over time you will read the whole book.

Have a go yourself. What have you got to lose?

This chapter has simply set out some general guidance for reading the Bible. Feel free to take from it what works for you. And don't forget that the goal with Bible reading is to become someone who reads all of scripture. Like the mother training her child to eat a well-balanced diet, you should slowly integrate more difficult books into your Bible reading. You'll first, however, need to become someone who regularly reads the Bible—ideally every day—and so you'll need to do what you can to cultivate that kind of reading habit.

A final thing to bear in mind is that reading the Bible can be a battle. The Bible teaches that there is an enemy of God— the Devil—and that he has many assistants. Their goal is to try and stop you from reading the Bible. As a result, there will be many obstacles in your way when you think you should be reading it. However, hopefully this book has instilled into you a feeling that the Bible is no ordinary book, and that you ought to do it justice and read it regularly. I am certain that if you approach the Bible with humility, and allow it to speak to you, it will change your life forever, and massively for the better.

Why not give it a go? You really should.